THE NARRATIVE PULSE OF *BEOWULF*:
ARRIVALS AND DEPARTURES

JOHN M. HILL

The Narrative Pulse
of *Beowulf*:
Arrivals and Departures

UNIVERSITY OF TORONTO PRESS
Toronto   Buffalo   London

Published by University of Toronto Press Incorporated
Toronto Buffalo London
Printed in Canada

ISBN 978-0-8020-9329-5

Printed on acid-free paper

Library and Archives Canada Cataloguing in Publication

Hill, John M.
  The narrative pulse of Beowulf : arrivals and departures / John M. Hill.

(Toronto Old English series)
Includes bibliographical references and index.
ISBN 978-0-8020-9329-5

1. Beowulf.   2. Epic poetry, English (Old) – History and criticism.   I. Title.
II. Series.

PR1585.H552 2008   829'.3   C2007-903501-9

University of Toronto Press acknowledges the financial assistance to
its publishing program of the Canada Council for the Arts and the
Ontario Arts Council.

University of Toronto Press acknowledges the financial support for its
publishing activities of the Government of Canada through the
Book Publishing Industry Development Program (BPIDP).

As always, for Barbara,
whose comings and goings are
the pulse of our life.

Contents

Acknowledgments

I wish to thank the several organizers of various sessions on *Beowulf* and Old English Literature in the recent past, where sections of this study first appeared as conference papers. They would include John D. Niles and Allen Frantzen. Marijane Osborn deserves special mention for inviting me to speak at the Davis Medieval Colloquium, where I was well received and where I met a number of fine students flourishing under her tutelage.

A portion of chapter 2 appeared in a somewhat altered form in *Beowulf in Our Time: Teaching Beowulf in Translation*. I am grateful to Mary K. Ramsey, who edited that volume, and to the Medieval Institute, Western Michigan University, for permission to republish from this Subsidia, vol. 31, of the Old English Newsletter.

I am enormously indebted to Suzanne Rancourt, of the University of Toronto Press, for immediately seeing value in my approach to the dramatic masterpiece that is *Beowulf*. The anonymous readers for the press were also very encouraging, generous in their praise, and quite insightful in their commentary. *The Narrative Pulse of* Beowulf is all the stronger for their help. Clare Orchard, the manuscript's copy editor, deserves a case of whatever is her favourite libation. She is superb. Among the press's other editors, I should note that Barb Porter has been meticulous in her instructions and genial in her postings.

Finally, I sadly regret that Stephen O. Glosecki, 'eaxlgesteallan minum,' is not here to tell me what is good and what needs more work. After terrible battles with the cancer demon, he has gone to Valhöll where, after sword play by day, I trust he now enjoys boar flesh and goat mead in the evening. In my own good time I hope to join in such feasting and even in the reciting of song. Steve has translated *Beowulf* into his own, stirring verse, such as this: 'Nevertheless, our wielding God, / Victory-Giver! Let him avenge himself; / with blade well edged was he brave alone'; and this, 'Ignoble deed! Death is better / than life without honor for any warrior!' Good from long ago, Steve had honour. Death came too soon.

THE NARRATIVE PULSE OF *BEOWULF*:
ARRIVALS AND DEPARTURES

The Narrative Pulse of *Beowulf*: Arrivals and Departures

There is much to be said for large-scale, structural views of *Beowulf*, beginning with Tolkien's view of the famous poem in two balanced parts (representing an 'opposition of ends and beginnings,' youth and age, and 'first achievement and final death'); or we might consider a three-part division, as say, H.L. Rogers, Kathryn Hume, John D. Niles, and others have suggested, focused on the three monster fights; or else, more capaciously, Gale R. Owen-Crocker's three movements and a coda fixed to the still points of four funerals 'from which thematic patterns radiate' within elliptical structures.[1] In story-line terms, that is, in ongoing, consequential narrative development and closure, the poem in fact clearly has two parts: the extended account of the Danish dynasty, beginning with Scyld Scefing and his departure, then Heorot's founding, Grendel's monstrous arrival, his repeated raids and years of night-time squatting; then Beowulf's arrival, his defeat of the monsters, his departure and triumphant return home: end of part one. We then have the final thousand lines or so about the awakening of the dragon, the approach and fight, and the sad aftermath. But large divisions of this sort fail to appreciate the narrative pulse scene by scene of the poem, which in fact carries right across the dragon divide to the very end, this second part of the poem seeming to many readers a falling off structurally. However, *Beowulf* is in fact a strongly narrative poem, contrary to Tolkien's sense, using Klaeber's phrase, that it lacks 'a steady advance.'

Above the level of stylistic variations and patterns, however described – whether we note chiastic structures, envelope patterns, ring patterns, interlace effects or 'digressive' jumps ahead and invited recollections of past kings and events, with both forward and backward shifts sometimes functioniong in fluid, interpretative ways – at the level of successive scenes, *Beowulf* is a poem of arrivals and departures, with lesser departures and arrivals inside major scenes, each one usually generating either social tension or expectation. Thus *Beowulf* is a poem of socially dramatic, often quite complex scenes galvanized by arrivals and defined in changing, dramatic moments by departures far more so than it is a poem of architecturally balanced oppositions, monster fights or the showcasing of a great hero who eventually dies in battle, leaving his people vulnerable to enemies he kept in check.[2]

When we consider Beowulf's departure from his people, the Geats, and his arrival on the Danish shore, we are actually in the process, a deeply social and always edgy process, of various arrivals. We are familiar with much of this; indeed most readers can readily list eleven or twelve scenes of notable arrival or departure, such as Beowulf's arrivals at the beach and in Heorot, Grendel's burst into Heorot and his mortally wounded departure, then the mother monster's sudden appearance and flight, Beowulf's departure into the lake and then his return, his leave-taking from Hrothgar, and his homecoming; then in part two the dragon's arrival, Beowulf's departure to seek the dragon, his arrival at the flame-emiting mound, and then his final departure as he confers war-band leadership upon Wiglaf. Although major scenes and rounded actions, these do not in themselves establish a steady, narrative pulse. At best they periodically pop up, however memorably, every 390 lines or so if we average them out across the poem. But when we highlight more than twenty scenes of arrival or departure, including approaches and returns or exits within some of them – as in Wealhtheow's movement away from, and then back to, Hrothgar after presenting the cup to Beowulf, and then Hrothgar's eventual exit; and when we consider the re-entrance of an already established character – as when Hrothgar and Wealhtheow approach Heorot, or when Beowulf enters Heorot the morning after Æschere's death, or when Beowulf arrives home, then the pulse of arrivals and departures notably quickens as it contracts between them, giving us such scenes on average every 150 lines. However, before moving in detail and at length into the poem's dramatic scenes, it is helpful to set out in overview first the many tensions or expectations that arise, and then the general sequencing of arrivals and departures from the beginning to the end of the poem.

Arrivals, especially unanticipated ones, are electric with possibilities, with unexpected surprises ranging from the pleasant and desired, the tense and potentially dangerous, to the terrible and unwished for. Expectations might be exploded; prospective trouble might erupt at any time. Beowulf's arrival on the beach is especially electric – potentially promising, potentially threatening, as are his successive arrivals at Heorot's portal, inside before Hrothgar and then on the meadbench among Hrothgar's retinue. Many more scenes of arrival will follow, as will scenes of departure. Departures are often auspicious, full of promise and hope, although they can also signify terror's monstrous flight. The latter clearly is the case for Grendel's departure after the fight, for his mother's retreat and, although still ominous, for the momentarily resting, perhaps regrouping dragon. Each human departure involves an enlargement of possibility, at least locally, with Beowulf's departure from the Danes being the most expansively promising in the poem. Even Beowulf's departure from the Geats the first time has an auspicious feel to it, wise men having read Beowulf's deep luck in their casting of signs. And his mood-darkened departure to fight the dragon, while heavy with the facts of night-time fury, has some promise in that an enraged Beowulf has armed himself carefully and the dragon's treasure is a mixed prospect to contemplate.

In all those moments either positive or negative outcomes are possible, indeed sometimes intertwining or sometimes just lurking as potential, either menacingly or frustratingly. They inform the social action of the poem even as the many arrivals and departures create its overall and variable narrative pulse. Some of this is unexceptionable, of course: the arrival of angry or aggrieved monsters is in effect the arrival of terror, their defeat or their departure something either to celebrate or contend with. But warrior arrivals and departures turn out to be socially complex affairs, not easily predictable or conventionally scripted. Therein lies their drama.

On an absolute scale of foundation stories, we have the arrival as an infant of Scyld Scefing among the Danes, presumably sometime after the expulsion and death of Heremod. That auspicious arrival, although Scyld is at first destitute, is summed up for us in his mature life by the poem's opening lines, which set up four generations of Danes – a narrated genealogy attaching fathers to sons and both to martial and cultural values, culminating in Hrothgar's ascension, his building of Heorot, and then the first, monstrous incursion. Among other things, that horrible arrival balances, so to speak, the first great departure – Scyld's ship-involved funeral after his long, successful reign. It also brings to at least a temporary close the generational continuations of Danish kingship and power, as first modelled restoratively in Scyld's activity, his warrior-king portrait and his successful son. Importantly the great affair that in effect arrives with Scyld is that restored model, one might even say myth, of Danish kingship. .

Often Scyld Scefing seized meadbenches from dangerous armies, from many peoples ('sceaþena þreatum, / monegum mægþum meodosetla ofteah,' ll. 4b–5).[3] He could do this because he was mightier, more terrifying – he in fact terrified noble warriors ('egsode eorl[as],' l. 6a) although he himself is not substantially a terror – as is Grendel the devourer. As it were, Scyld's terror is channelled, becoming a martial and social value rather than remaining simply a terrible affair. However, 'egsian,' 'to terrify,' rests uneasily within the poem's words for all that is terrible, fearful, horrible ('egesa,' 'egesfull,' 'egeslic'). Those words quite often apply either as simplexes or compounds equally to Grendel and the dragon or to their habitats or habits (one of several notable exceptions is in line 1827a, where Beowulf offers aid should he learn that surrounding peoples threaten or terrify the Danes – the terror of neighbours noted again in 2736; Beowulf then is the poem's supreme guardian against, and exterminator of, terror). But in Scyld's case such activity is martial consolation for an orphaned beginning, when he was found, a wretched waif. Waging war, he prospered in honour and glory ('weorðmyndum þah,' 8b), such that, or until, each surrounding tribe gave him tribute. That was a good king, a judgment offered without irony by the poet. So this is the cultural model of a major battle-king: he subdues his neighbours, wrecking their halls and terrifying their warriors until they sue for peace and a tribute-paying relationship with him. In this way he protects his people and he and they prosper both in their military activities, given what they seize or plunder, and in the tribute they accumulate. That matter of tribute ('gombe') is important. For a king like Scyld Scefing would be too formidable, even unapproachable, if he did not accept tribute, if instead he simply triumphed over others and gathered plundered wealth. Tribute is a reciprocal affair here, evident in the verb 'gyldan,' to pay or repay (rightly, ethically). Defeated hall-troops and their kings repay Scyld's generosity in letting them live after he has terrorized them; they may even in paying tribute to Scyld keep some of their wealth and their fortified places (as do the inhabitants of Sodom in the

Old English *Genesis*, although after twelve years they rebel against their Viking overlords – ll. 1976–81); moreover, implicitly Scyld protects his tribute-bearing subjects.

But when such a king dies those very people and their clients may well then exact retribution if they can. At this point the most important aspect of the Scyld model comes into play. Only the advent of a powerful, war-like successor can forestall or else prevent such retribution and indeed show forth the king's essential favouring by God or the gods. Because such an advent is not something a mighty king can insure for himself, the birth of strong, generous sons is like a God-given blessing. In Scyld's case that is what happens in the birth of the Danish Beowulf (Beowulf I, not the poem's hero). The poet assigns divine blessing to this birth – a son sent as solace to the Danes who had earlier suffered without a lord (before Scyld Scefing arrived and prospered). This rise of Beowulf I in effect repairs a pattern broken down with Heremod's abuse of prosperity, for which he receives exile and death. So continuity and succession in strong kings is not something a people can count on; its appearance is a divine blessing underwriting the cultural value of prosperous succession, which depends on military strength and activity, in turn being dependent on the generosity of the battle lord. The young Beowulf (I) proves himself a capable warrior and generous leader, winning fame and attracting retainers ('on fæder bearme,' l. 21b) while his powerful father still lives (which also softens the father, so to speak, by moving his war-like activities onto the next generation). 'So should a young man do! By famous deeds shall, among peoples anywhere, a man *prosper*' (as Beowulf I's father does – thus 'þeon' [ll. 8, 25] marks a two-generational model, that is, myth, of kingship). The poet's approval of this is unqualified and sets up the spectacle without fear, although not without grief, of Scyld's death, the poem's first great departure.

'[Þ]æt wæs god cyning;' 'Swa sceal (geong g)uma gode gewyrcean'; 'lofdædum sceal / in mægþa gehwære man geþeon' (ll. 11b; 20; 24b–25). The cultural beat of these twenty-five lines is sententious, that of the maxim. The death and ship funeral for Scyld follows immediately after, as though keyed triumphantly and ritually to the idea of prospering. Scyld's own retainers lay their beloved lord into the ship, which, ice-covered and partly anthropomorphized, is eager to set out, to carry Scyld into the Lord's protection. This winter funeral includes piling extraordinary weapons and treasures around Scyld's body and setting a golden banner overhead. Scyld came to the Danes in the beginning impoverished, a baby; he leaves them, an old, powerful king, much honoured and spectacularly accompanied by riches, although his mourners, whether counsellors or warriors, do not know who or what received (or took) that load – that is, where he arrived in death.

Departure here is auspicious if not altogether certain in the matter of afterlife voyaging, for Scyld's Beowulf (I) now rules, a beloved people's king, his fame widespread; from him awakens a powerful son in turn, Healfdene, who will rule long, aged and battle-fierce. Thus the overlapping, two-generational Scyld model, as it were, is implicitly reproduced in the next father-son pair: a powerful, generous and prosperous battle king has a healthy son and is softened by that son's military prowess, which in turn returns us to something of the fierceness in Scyld Scefing. This alternation of fierce king and able but less battle-fierce, more legislative king (in that warriors come to him and he is beloved), fills out the model of kingship as an institution, the alternation refreshing in turn each aspect of successful kingship – sheer war-power and generous, legislative power, that generosity including the giving of gifts and the attracting of warriors. From the fierce Healfdene, who apparently is maritally vigorous, arise four children – three sons and a daughter, Hrothgar among them (to whom victory and honour in war are given, 'wiges weorðmynd' [l. 65a] such that men eagerly serve him). Presumably Hrothgar's older brother also fulfils the model, making this now three-times incarnated model effectively a Danish myth of kingship, something more, then, than just a lineal establishing of a fortunate, four-generation dynasty, presumably divinely blest. As a myth of kingship, its efficacy is in the need to re-enact and refresh its dimensions across each two-generational succession – father to son, while the father lives; son becomes father with a son or sons of his own. Failure to do so may have unhappy consequences.

Healfdene's daughter apparently is given to Onela, a Swedish king who will eventually cause the Geats some pain when he attacks them in search of his exiled, rebellious nephews. This mention of Onela is the first indication in the poem of alliances between peoples rather than of the subjugation of surrounding tribes. As such it marks an opening out into the world rather than a singular focus on the Danish house and its line of powerful descent. Women are marriage bonds between groups; only through their sons can they participate in the model of kingship sketched above, assuming that those sons grow into resourceful, war-band leaders.

Hrothgar, then, in the poem's movement of successive adverbs, is given success in war. Apparently his battle skills earn him the kingship as well over Halga, his younger brother, who along with other kinsmen eagerly listened to him ('þæt him his winemagas / georne hyrdon,' 65b–66a). These Danish youths grew, maturing into a large cohort of warrior kinsmen, and so the myth seems happily incarnated again, although Hrothgar is not said to have prospered while his powerful, older brother lived. When, later, Hrothgar mentions coming into the kingship (ll. 467–9) after Heorogar dies, there saying he (Heorogar) was better than Hrothgar, he probably does not mean that Heorogar was a greater battle king; rather, first, Heorogar never faced anything like the suffering Hrothgar by that point has experienced in the Grendel affair; thus he and his kingship were better than Hrothgar and his. Secondly, and perhaps more deeply, Heorogar, having no powerful son or sons, deviates from the myth of Danish kingship without bad consequences (thus having better luck). Hrothgar, apparently, has not avoided grave developments – his sons are too young to take on some of his martial spirit anytime soon, thus softening him and refreshing the battle-fierce dimension of kingship, and Grendel has in the meantime stricken Hrothgar and polluted the night-time life of the hall.

Perhaps in some obscure, Germanic sense, this, more than any explicable show of pride or fratricidal sin or whatever, is what awakens the monster – deviation from the myth, even if simply a matter of fortune, calls out the night-time usurper of the hall, the horrible squatter. In this connection we should recall what is said of Heremod, that his people hoped he would take on his father's excellence ('fæderæþelum,' l. 911a) and properly hold the people, treasure, and strong-place. That he does not do so is an absolute, personal violation of the myth, for which there is the retribution of exile and death. We will return to this myth of kingship and to the central attributes it enshrines for any king from a more expansive, anthropological perspective in chapter 3. For now we should follow Hrothgar for a time and then move from this opening to complete our overview of the poem's arrivals and departures.

Inspired by the idea of building a great hall and naming it Heorot, Hrothgar proceeds to command just that – a hall named Heorot rises, in which Hrothgar plans to distribute to young and old alike all that God has given him, except for the folk-commons and the lives of men (fulfilling the legislative side of kingship). The towering hall and the joy and song of men within it now attract the poem's first, baleful arrival – Grendel, the devastating, night-time raider. As anticipated above, readers have worried much over what attracts him: has Hrothgar somehow grown proud, in need of punishment? Does he need a brutal scorning on his meadbenches, which in the morning, if nocturnally occupied by Danes, steam with blood and gore (Grendel having wandered off mysteriously with his booty)? This deeply damaged creature ('wiht unhælo') comes and goes, exulting in his slaughter. He does not come as a guest, although he is initially called 'se ellengæst' (l. 86a – the topological similarity of *gæst* and *gast* and *gist* can confuse editors and readers).[4] Thus his first arrival does not create tension, although surely his second one does, when he triumphs again in his murderous way. It becomes obvious, pointed and said truly in the clear sign ('sweotolan tacne,' l. 141b) of the 'hall-thane's' hate, that one who would escape the fiend should seek rest elsewhere than in Heorot.

Grendel strives against right in his feud and crime – for which he never offers compensation or surcease; he thus definitively stands outside the possibility of ethical settlement (which suggests that an unrighteous pride is not what has called him out). More than anything else, and moreover coming not as guest but as something ghastly, a monstrous hall-thane – that is why Grendel cannot approach the gift-seat, the treasure, because of God: 'no he þone gifstol gretan moste, / maþðum for Metode, ne his myne wisse,' ll. 168–9; nor can he know Hrothgar's welcoming or questioning or expectant thoughts, whose gift seat after all it is – this even though Grendel occupies Heorot at night. Obviously he does not have royal permission – unlike later, when Beowulf, his nemesis, is given special guardianship of the hall, in which he will meet Grendel and eventually produce a reciprocal, an answering, sign of victory ('tacen sweotol,' l. 833b) – Grendel's disembodied arm and shoulder. In a sense, the treasure in Heorot, principally Hrothgar's gift seat, is something the squatter-like Grendel would possess in his night-time having. God prevents that because no one else can – perhaps a sign in this deep trouble and dark time that God is somehow on Hrothgar's side, although not on the side of those unnamed Danes who invoke a demon-slayer in their heathen despair over Grendel.[5]

Eventually word of Grendel's deeds reaches Hygelac's great thane, a good man among the Geats; he was of mankind the strongest in might in those days of this life, noble and huge. Seemingly, Beowulf the Geat decides impulsively to seek Hrothgar, that war-king who has need of men. Is his quest simply for glory, despite the great risk? Or is there something in the idea of 'need' that a right-minded, ethical warrior cannot ignore? We will return to this in the next chapter. For now it is enough to note that soon after Beowulf's decision Grendel, in his night-time occupation, and in a series of expressive movements that some readers have treated as designed impact and irony, as well as finding them psychologically and perceptually effective, will certainly approach the wrong bench.[6] In what will very soon become more Beowulf's story than anyone else's, there are many arrivals and departures, which we can now skirt round before analysing them individually in their social contexts. However, what has already been established in the poem about notable departures and arrivals is their scope, the display of great success in one case and the advent of great terror in the other. Along with that is a sense of the inexplicable, of dark if not always portentous mysteries: men do not know from whence Scyld came or who or what takes or receives Scyld and his glittering funeral ship; nor do men know where those who are skilled in the mysteries of hell go in their gliding and turning movements (said of that 'helrune,' l. 163a, Grendel) – or for all that, why they come.

With Beowulf, matters are clearer as the pulse of arrivals and departures now begins to quicken; moreover, we can say that in fact Beowulf arrives among the Danes and departs several times: first on the beach, to be challenged by the coast watch; from there he departs with the coast watch's blessing and escort, who will also set a guard for Beowulf's ship; escorted by the coastguard, Beowulf then arrives at Heorot, met by Wulfgar, who departs to inform Hrothgar of the arrival of armed strangers, noting that one of them is extraordinary and calls himself Beowulf; then Beowulf and his retinue arrive inside the great hall, before Hrothgar, Wealhtheow, Unferth, and others. He asks for permission to deal with Grendel, eventually receives it and occupies the hall for the night, after Hrothgar and his warriors regally depart. The next morning it is Hrothgar and Wealhtheow who arrive, before whom Beowulf recounts his efforts. That next night, after gift giving and celebration in Heorot, Grendel's mother arrives, is frightened, grabs a warrior and departs. The next morning, Beowulf arrives again at the hall, having evidently slept elsewhere after the celebrations; when informed of the surprising, terrible thing that has happened, he states his military resolve and he and Hrothgar then depart with their retainers to hunt down Grendel's mother. They arrive near mere's edge and stare in pain at Æschere's severed head; then they stir up angry sea-dragons, killing and landing one, before Beowulf prepares to depart into those forbidding waters. He eventually arrives at the bottom of the mere where Grendel's mother grabs him and takes him into her underwater hall, from which he eventually emerges victorious, arriving again at surface level and then back in Heorot, from which again, after more meditative speeches and celebration, he prepares to depart the following morning. That departure is socially momentous in that Beowulf offers Hrothgar a personal alliance, one that Hrothgar turns into a grand alliance between Geats and Danes (but more on that later). Beowulf then goes to his ship, rewards the Dane there guarding it, and leaves, arriving soon enough on the beach near where his uncle and lord rules from within a great hall. That arrival is socially momentous as well, culminating in great amity between Beowulf and Hygelac, who bestows a rich, sub-kingship upon Beowulf.

Some fifty winters later the dragon arrives on a fateful night and scorches the settlement, Beowulf's hall, and the surrounding lands. Beowulf, finding the thief who knows the way to the dragon's mound, leaves the settlement and arrives outside the barrow, from which flames still issue. Here he sits down, having already had uncustomary, dark thoughts. Now, sad and restless, eager for slaughter as well, he feels the nearness of fate. He offers an apologia for himself and his life before departing from his men to challenge the dragon. In the course of that fight, when Beowulf is surrounded by flames and forced to retreat, Wiglaf arrives to help him. Together they kill the dragon, after which Wiglaf departs to rummage through the dragon's mound for a huge armload of treasure Beowulf can see before he dies (that treasure signifying his wergeld to Beowulf). Beowulf then dies, but not before conferring something like war-band leadership on Wiglaf. Beowulf's other retainers now arrive and receive Wiglaf's fierce rebuke. Wiglaf then sends a messenger to the Geat warriors who did not accompany Beowulf. The messenger arrives with bad news and not very good expectations of the future. Following that, many Geats leave with the messenger to see the doleful sight of dead king and dragon for themselves. Arriving, they find Beowulf and Wiglaf, who then addresses them, commenting on Beowulf's high destiny, reinforcing the messenger's tenor and also ordering the making of a bier and the building of a funeral pyre. While he offers bad news, Wiglaf's relation to the Geats has become socially notable and his status has greatly changed now that he is not just a member of Beowulf's retinue.

That narrative pulse of sometimes terrible, sometimes promising if potentially threatening arrivals and sometimes hopeful departures seems to be the poem's own. When reviewed as above, comprehensively, that the *Beowulf* narrative moves along some such pulse soon seems obvious enough, perhaps even unexceptionably so. After all, the poem has many scenes, and scenes typically – as with type-scenes – have frames, beginnings and ends, thresholds, sometimes conventional motifs, and at least temporary resolutions. However, the scenes in *Beowulf* of arrival and departure are highly dramatic, with arrivals initiating response and action, while departures mark significant changes in the hopes or expectations or even the status of interacting characters. In this *Beowulf* is virtually, startlingly unique among Northern poems from the early middle ages. To gauge that uniqueness we should now turn to whatever potential parallels suggest themselves before bringing this introductory overview to a close, and before exploring further the poem's deeper story-structure, across which the narrative is organized and driven.

In comparison to European stories, whether northern or Germanic, or classical and Mediterranean, the narrative pulse of *Beowulf* more nearly approximates comings and goings in Homeric epics than the incident structure of northern sagas and histories, or else the arrival scenes of the *Aeneid*. It is significant too that *Beowulf* has no close parallels in these matters even among Old English poems. There is some conversational testing in *Andreas*: the hero needs passage across the sea for himself and his men; coming upon a ship and its crew, he engages the apparent master (Christ in disguise) and asks for help, even though he has no money for his fare. Earlier he has been challenged about wanting to go to a land where death is likely: 'ond þu wilnast nu ofer widne mere, / þæt ðu on þa fægðe þine feore spilde'?[7] Implicitly, is Andreas a fool; would he throw his life away? Andreas sidesteps the implication and simply asserts sharp desire ('usic lust hweteð'): he and his men feel compelled to reach that famous city. Apparently such desire is self-explanatory – the kind that motivates the speaker in the *Seafarer*, for example. But on the matters of payment and provisioning, Christ (still unrevealed) challenges Andreas again:

'Hu geweard þe þæs, wine leofesta, / ðæt ðu sæbeorgas secan woldes, / merestreama gemet, maðmum bedæled/ ... Is se drohtað strang / þam þe lagolade lange cunnaþ' (307–14). Implicitly, Andreas is accused of silliness at least – 'my *dear* man' – and reckless foolhardiness at most – the concluding maxim implying an overlooked wisdom – that he would attempt an arduous sea voyage without provisions of any kind. Andreas replies directly (loosely): 'it is not fitting for one to whom the Lord has given much in the way of goods and worldly success that you answer me in such proud and grievous terms; it is better [his answering maxim] that one humbly or joyfully acknowledges the man eager to go elsewhere, as Christ has commanded.' He then goes on to identify his divinely commanded mission and receives Christ's permission to board. The overall context for these and further exchanges is mainly a test of Andreas's faith and beliefs, which tumble out directly enough. The scene is not electric with possibilities, or with untoward surprises.[8]

Among prose texts, the fulsome welcoming scenes in *Apollonius of Tyre* hardly count; only once in fact is a note of tension introduced, on the part of an envious counsellor, who negatively characterizes Apollonius's countenance at a banquet, suggesting to the king that Apollonius, because sadly gazing at everything and saying nothing, is envious of the king's wealth. The king immediately corrects or chastens the counsellor: Apollonius behaves as he does because he has suffered great loss. And so an Unferth-like possibility is crushed in the very run of syntax that raised it. Outside of Old English literary texts, we can look to Asser's life of King Alfred for how generously that king thinks to provide for visitors and strangers; however, we will find very little in those passages to parallel with *Beowulf*, apart, perhaps, from Hygelac's welcoming of his sister's son. Looking in another direction, to Anglo-Saxon laws, we can in fact gather some sense of affairs that approximate some of the tensions in *Beowulf*, especially if we focus on the codicils that are generally wary of and sometimes almost hostile toward strangers. Indeed, the laws may well give us documentary, legislative context for this aspect of our poem – a possibility I will return to at the end of this study. Keeping ourselves to Old English poetical texts or to literary prose, then, we have found little to compare with in the corpus. However, looking to the Mediterranean, to Homer especially, will bring some surprisingly close parallels into focus.

Although separated notably by time, culture, and geography, and while there is no direct influence, the *Beowulf* poet and Homer dramatize some similar, anthropologically parallel institutions – especially the host-guest relationship, that is, the initial tensions of hospitality and their generous developments when matters go well. One might even say that in this respect and in the patterns of arrivals and departures, *Beowulf* is an enveloped, much shorter, first nine books of the *Odyssey* – an Anglo-Saxon odyssey of course. Some readers since the beginning of *Beowulf* scholarship, no doubt because of their classical training and their interest in raising the poem to comparative, classical standing, have noted similarities between episodes in *The Odyssey* and in *Beowulf*; indeed, as Theodore Andersson reminds us, perhaps 'there is at least some residual illumination of the *Beowulf* poet's sensibilities implicit in the oddity that almost all the comparisons [with Homer] have paired *Beowulf* with the *Odyssey* rather than the *Iliad*.'[9] That 'oddity' may simply reflect the classical education of earlier scholars; they hit upon resemblances between texts they know well and they also want their poem, *Beowulf*, to have some pride of place among the Western world's great epics (something Germanicists especially may have wanted). However, some of those readers may have sensed genuine similarities but did not look into the social worlds within the poems carefully enough to ground that sense in anything other than formal episodes. Recently Carolyn Anderson has pointed out an arresting parallel in the area of host-guest tensions.

Even in a nominally peaceful meeting, danger can come from either party; the social rules naming obligations and appropriate behaviours for both parties are a means of subduing that conflict. The rituals of ' household ceremonies ... convert the stranger from a nonentity and prey to a person with status. Hostility to a stranger is both natural and monstrous. Polyphemus, that uncivil monster, did not entertain his guests; he ate them ... if it were not for the restraints of civility, man would become to man as predator to prey' (Redfield). There are ritualized greetings, asking the stranger to 'tell of himself, his land, and his ancestry' (Odyssey 19. 104–5). Gifts to the stranger 'provide outsiders, who are by nature without status, with that place in society which constitutes an identity' (Murnaghan). In Greek culture, Zeus is the 'Ξείνιος', the 'Protector of strangers,' and the choice of supreme god for this role marks the cultural importance of the social dilemma.[10]

More germane to Beowulf's initial arrival on the Danish coast, and the coast watch's challenge, would be those moments in *The Odyssey* when a seafarer arrives: Nestor asks Telemachus, 'Where did you sail from, over the running sea-lanes? / Out on a trading spree or roving the waves like pirates, / sea-wolves raiding at will, who risk their lives to plunder other men.'[11] In Book 9 the Cyclops asks virtually the same question and in Book 7, Alcinous's queen, Arete of the hospitable Phaeacians, sharply questions the stranger (Odysseus): 'Who are you? Where are you from? / Who gave you the clothes you're wearing now? / Didn't you say you reached us roving on the sea.'[12] This stranger might be a thief on land and a rover pirate at sea.[13] In Book 8, Odysseus is insulted for his apparent lack of athleticism or of interest in sports: 'You're some skipper of profiteers, / roving the high seas in his scudding craft, / reckoning up his freight with a keen eye out / for home cargo, grabbing the gold he can! / You're no athlete' (ll. 186–90). A noble warrior would not be a grubby sea-merchant or a profiteer's captain; he would invest in the excellence of competition. After the angry Odysseus shows stunning prowess, the speaker later apologizes and presents Odysseus with a fine sword, while hoping the gods will grant the stranger safe passage home. Odysseus in turn calls him friend and wishes god-granted good fortune for him as well. The parallel in *Beowulf*, noted by James Work (1930), is the Unferth episode, although the latter is much more complex.

Then there is a possibility, not in keeping with good behaviour, that the prepossessing strangers who have just arrived by chariot (Telemachus and Pisistratus, Nestor's son) might be shunted off to someone else. Menelaus, greatly offended by the suggestion, considers it a childish, boorish one. Yet it suggests tension in that the strangers might not be worthy and the cost of hosting them might be constraining. Aside from the Cyclops encounter, all of the others end well and in some way are enriching or auspicious for the stranger when he leaves: Telemachus gets help and finally a sybil's news through Menelaus of his father, alive but somehow bespelled by Calypso; Odysseus is sent off in an incredibly swift ship, loaded with fine provisions, to Ithaca (although Poseidon's revenge is very bad for the Phaeacians).

One might add parallels from various places in both Homeric poems, such as the embassy to Achilles in Book IX of *The Iliad* where Achilles answers in order points set out in Odysseus's speech and where the idea that men distinguish themselves both by fighting well and speaking well appears in Phoenix's reply to Achilles. Odysseus, Ajax, and Phoenix are stunned by what Achilles has just spoken, 'struck dumb – Achilles' ringing denials overwhelmed them so.'[14]

Eventually Achilles' old mentor and charioteer, Phoenix, finds his voice in a burst of tears and fear: 'Sail home? Is *that* what you're turning over in your mind ... The old horseman Peleus had me escort you, / that day he sent you out of Phithia to Agamemnon, / a youngster still untrained for the great leveler, war, / still green at debate where men can make their mark. / So he dispatched me, to teach you all these things, / to make you a man of words and a man of action too.' The words and deeds formula in *Beowulf*, much noted by various readers, here quite clearly has an Iliadic parallel in questioned context: how could a warrior so accomplished in both words and deeds now utter what Achilles has just uttered? This is a great shock and a sorrow for Phoenix, the Beowulfian parallel perhaps being the asserted advice, off-stage, that Wiglaf says he and others gave when Beowulf prepared to set out and greet the dragon (leave dragons gone to their lairs alone).

Then there is the ever present danger, despite divine preparations, that something Priam says will spur Achilles' anger in Book 24, who even in defiance of Zeus might then kill his suppliant guest, Priam. This danger becomes overt when the urgent Trojan king would have Achilles return Hector's body: 'Give him back to me, now, no more delay – / I must see my son with my own eyes. / Accept the ransom I bring you, a king's ransom! / Enjoy it, all of it – return to your own native land, safe and sound ... since now you've spared my life.'[15] Achilles replies powerfully, 'don't tempt my wrath, not now! / My mind's made up to give you back your son ... So don't anger me now. Don't stir my raging heart still more. / Or under my own roof I may not spare your life, old man – / suppliant that you are – may break the laws of Zeus' (lines 666–9). There is no obvious parallel to these moments in *Beowulf*, although as petitioners Beowulf and his Geats cannot be sure they will receive the boon Beowulf hopes for; and the thief who brought the dragon's ancient, ornamented cup to Beowulf might have wondered about how he would be received.

It is in matters such as these – in host-guest relationships, in gift giving, and in the protocols of house and hospitality – that the two poets operate in anthropologically similar, although far from identical, worlds (the ancient Greek having clan-based kinship patterns, something the Anglo-Saxons do not). However, in the northern poem there is always the demand, finally, that deeds and gifts be reciprocated, rather than loaded upon the stranger and thus given away, although in the Homeric cases an indirect reciprocity holds in that in his turn the stranger, if he has means, would do the same. Moreover, in *Beowulf* one must reveal oneself – either directly or else be revealed by the narrator in such a way as to be known to all. Although Unferth does not give his name, Beowulf knows, as we do, who he is. In *Beowulf* the stranger is not divinely protected and all that is honourable is public – no secrets, no disguises. But the status of the guest is that of the stranger ('gast, giest, gist') and is associatively, if not etymologically, in confusable proximity with the meaning and status of the evildoer or 'gæst.' We should now turn back to *Beowulf* and its scenes of arrivals and departures, which of course are largely the reflexes of Tolkien's two-phase Beowulf story inside a Danish opening. How the story becomes two phases should, however, delay us a little.

The poet has combined in complex ways at least two, great phases in Beowulf's life. Perhaps the mid- to late nineteenth-century theories, especially that of Karl Müllenhoff, about hero tales by different hands somehow stitched together into the epic we have are not altogether foolish. They can give us little sense of the poem we now read and are impossibly subjective when stipulating what 'lays' and other material must have pre-existed the poem and how and when they were added.[16] However, the poem itself suggests a library shelf of tales, let's say cycles, involving both Danish princes and kings (with notable analogues in northern story-telling) and Geatish ones, the synthesizing bridge or else anticipatory scribal move between the two plausibly being the two Beowulfs, the Dane – son of Scyld Scefing (and in some Anglo-Saxon genealogies known as Beow being the son of Scyld, son of Shef), and father of Healfdene, who father's Hrothgar among others – and the Geat, son of Hygelac's sister, eventual purge-warrior of Hrothgar's hall, Heorot.[17]

The *Beowulf* poet has dramatically combined these two lines of story into one that favours, so to speak, the Geat cycle, which we might say is mainly the Beowulf cycle: stories of his youth, adolescence, early manhood, full manhood, and old age may have existed as oral narratives. If they did, about eleven stories have been brilliantly combined, elegantly compressed, incorporated, and synthesized into aspects of the poem we have, often given to us economically through speeches, digressions, asides, and either brief recollections or extended, competing stories. (1) As a seven-year-old,

Beowulf is fostered by Hrethel and witnesses at least the sad aftermath of his foster family's tragedy: Hæðcyn's accidental slaying of
his brother; (2) Soon after, although perhaps not considered very
promising, he may have gone along as a young camp attendant on
Hygelac's rescue expedition to Ravenswood; (3) as an adolescent
he and an aspiring Bronding companion challenge each other to
difficult feats of swimming with swords, with different accounts
eventually circulating of how their extreme recreations ended –
Beowulf's including the slaughter of orally predatory sea beasts; (4)
later he avenges injuries to the Geats by the gruelling destruction of
five sea monsters; (5) as a frighteningly powerful, monster-slaying
champion and still young, he undertakes his propitious mission to
the Danes; (6) as a fully tested and rewarded retainer, a sub-king, he
would have accompanied Hygelac either as advance party or as
point man in the v-shaped shield wall during various raids perhaps
mainly among the Franks and Frisians; (7) as a worthy sub-king, he
accompanies Hygelac on an ill-fated raid among the Frisians and
Franks again, where he destroys the Frankish-Hugan champion and
that champion's entire war band; (8) as that victor, but returning
without his dear uncle and lord, he faces an offer of the kingship,
formally presented in a surprising way by Hygd, Hygelac's young
queen; instead he supports his cousin, her son; (9) then there is the
story of his cousin and king, generously entangled in a Swedish
family revolt, being killed by Onela, the Swedish king and probably
Hrothgar's son-in-law, while Beowulf apparently is somewhere else
although eventually favoured as king by Onela. Perhaps Beowulf is
securing the Waegmunding inheritance against Onela's possible
appropriation given that Weohstan, Wiglaf's father, fights for Onela
against Onela's nephews and Beowulf is the saviour of the Danes,
Onela's in-laws; (10) Beowulf then becomes king and avenges his
cousin's death by aiding a surviving Swedish contender (Eadgils)
against that contender's uncle, Onela again; (11) as an old man
Beowulf fatefully engages an enraged, hoard-guarding dragon
stirred up by a thief. By putting these eleven stories together in the
course of various expositions, and by dramatically emphasizing
aspects of them through individual speeches and monologues, while
greatly expanding and socially complicating the stories of early
manhood and old age, we might say that the *Beowulf* poet has picked
out the fifth and the eleventh for a sophisticated narrative develop-

ment of arrivals and departures that, for social drama, both Tolkien and Shakespeare could appreciate. The chapters that follow will develop those events as they arise out of arrivals and lead to departures in all of their changing social gesture, surprise, and expectation.

CHAPTER TWO

Beowulf's Sudden Arrival and Danish Challenges: Nothing Said Is Merely a Formality

Beowulf, perhaps in part impetuous and ambitious, no sooner hears of Grendel's deeds, news that must include the long duration of Danish suffering, than he decides to help. He, the strongest warrior in those days of this life, noble and huge, would seek the battle king over the swan-road because he, that battle king, is in 'need' (þearf) of men. Aside from personal ambition and the lure of glory, the socially compelling possibility for Beowulf is that the illustrious lord and battle king, Hrothgar, is in need. Here 'need' can mean simply something to fear, as in a dire need; but a need for men has ethical weight, as in the point much later that Beowulf has armed and gifted his retainers in the event that he should ever need help, which he does against the dragon, as Wiglaf says (ll. 2637 and following). Responding to that need is something of which the poet deeply approves, pronouncing Wiglaf a thane at, in the event of, need ('þegn æt ðearfe,' l. 2709). His lord's dire need calls Wiglaf forward, almost impulsively.

But to return to the young Beowulf, feeling an ethical call – which he will formulate in the same way again when promising an alliance in the course of taking his final leave of Hrothgar – Beowulf must now materially act upon it. Apparently he is well enough established that he can command maritime resources, have a ship prepared for his journey. Moreover, his prospective journey becomes auspiciously invested. Wise men among the Geats do not blame even a little his stepping out although he is beloved by them; they cast omens, apparently good ones, and so they whet the valiant one. Beowulf, then, hears a kind of free-warrior duty call, in that he is not Hrothgar's thane, and his valiant proposal is urged by wise men. Glory has yet to enter into this developing equation, unless it is implicit in his desire to help a glorious, famous, and illustrious lord.

Beowulf then picks a troop of bold, keen companions – fifteen of the best he can find – before setting out to the land of the Danes. Clearly Beowulf does not need permission to do what he has done, although wise men ('snotere ceorlas') have paused over their beloved warrior's idea long enough to say nothing against it and to cast an omen about his luck and safety ('hæl sceawedon,' l. 204b) – apparently a brilliant cast penetrating deeply to the truth of Beowulf's life until, that is, he faces the dragon. At that time he will hope for better luck and better circumstances for his beloved retainers than he seems to have drawn for himself.

Upon sighting gleaming sea cliffs and wide headlands, the Geats head for shore and land. So far we have seen the outsized Beowulf in command of a ship, its gathered, warrior crew and its military provisioning. They have a safe crossing but Beowulf has not sent ambassadors ahead: he arrives with his ship of heavily armed men, unannounced. As they climb out we are told their chain mail shirts resounded or clattered, their war gear ('syrcan hrysedon, / guðgewædo,' ll. 226b–227a). That sound cannot have escaped any nearby, Danish shore patrol, even as the Geats then thank God because the voyage has been easy. Easy but to what purpose? Basic friendliness is not yet called for – rather a strong challenge in an edgy social situation comes first from Hrothgar's coast watch.[1]

As Tom Shippey notes, a 'face threatening act' occurs here, managed by the coast watch, in whom an intense curiosity roils ('hine fyrwyt bræc / modgehygdum,' ll. 232b–233a) as to just who these men are.[2] Shippey applies modern theory about conversational principles to Beowulfian exchanges, as much to test the universal applicability of those principles as taken from Grice, Leach, and others as to explore the ways in which speech conventions operate differently in this representation of an archaic, warrior world when compared to our own, middle-class set. So: the coast watch rides down boldly to the shore, brandishing a mighty spear in his hand. Because shaking a mighty spear, his words of 'counsel' ('meþelword') are basically battle words: 'Who are you who come thus armed openly across the waves' ('Hwæt syndon ge searohæbbendra, / byrnum werede, þe þus brontne ceol / ofer lagustræte lædan cwomon / hider ofer holmas?' ll. 237a–240a). Obviously this ship has carried no soft-weeded merchants. The coastguard's forward question, as Shippey notes, is then ameliorated somewhat by his statement of who he is and why he challenges them. He is stationed there at the frontier to guard against enemies who come by ship. This should surely go without saying; but what is not conversationally obvious is what he might think the new arrivals portend – are they the advance party for a large force still at sea? They have come, he says, quite familiarly; moreover, they know they lack the permission of warriors or the consent of kinsmen. Yet they come openly, bearing their shields: are they friendly or unusually bold, he implies? 'No her cuðlicor cuman ongunnon / lindhæbbende, ne ge leafnesword / guðfremmendra gearwe ne wisson, / maga gemedu' (ll. 244–247a). Still, the coast watch adds, he has never seen a greater nobleman on the earth than is one among them, a warrior in armour, honoured by weapons; never may his peerless countenance belie him. Appearances can be deceiving; trust can be badly placed – all implications of 'næfne him his wlite leoge' (250b). Expectations can be bitterly, grievously belied by subsequent revelations and events. Although the coast watch has here already singled out the huge warrior for special attention, and expressed a guarded conditional, he has not addressed and thus challenged him directly.

Now, he says somewhat urgently, he will know who they are, their lineage, before they proceed further into the land of the Danes, possible marauders on reconnaissance ('leassceaweras,' l. 253a). He all but orders them to reveal themselves to him quickly – whence have you come? His manner is bold, potentially insulting – the insult tempered by the clear thought he wants them to heed ('anfealdne geþoht,' l. 256a): 'haste is best to reveal whence you have come.' Yet he has stated his grounds for challenging them: they come with no prior permission nor do they sport kinship recognition. Tom Shippey, in his 1993 landmark account of conversational gambits in *Beowulf*, perceptively analysed the coast watch's performance here in terms of a 'conflictive principle' – where one must establish one's worth, have it acknowledged, be prepared to acknowledge the other's worth or, if not, respond 'with an appropriate degree of reciprocal non-acknowledgment.'[3] I accept Shippey's basic characterization of this conversational exchange and acknowledge that he does not have room in his 1993 essay to explore the nuances of what Beowulf says in reply to the coast watch. My contribution here is just that – to explore those nuances as Beowulf's way of matching something to nearly everything the coast watch has said. Nothing goes completely unnoted, although the noting may well in this social world be indirect.[4]

The most prominent among them, as should be expected, will answer him: he, their chief, says they are men of the Geats, Hygelac's hearth-retainers. Thus initially Beowulf reveals their general, tribal affiliation along with their war-band allegiance. This is an immediate, open concession. Without giving his name, he proceeds to identify his father, Ecgtheow, who lived long and is widely known – thus specifying a personal kinship tie and suggesting that surely the coast watch knows of Ecgtheow. And surely Beowulf knows that Hrothgar recruited Ecgtheow long ago, settling a feud on his behalf. In these remarks Beowulf indirectly answers the issue of kinship ties – there is connection here, albeit a constructed one in the past, in terms of the recruited kinship of the war-band. Given that Ecgtheow is well known and was recruited by Hrothgar, by implication the leader now and his retainers have come in similarly open, friendly terms – not in secret on a raid. So much for now about who they are and from where they have come. Beowulf does not feel he needs to be more specific with the coast watch – such as giving his exact family relationship to Hygelac (sister's son) or his also social relationship to Hrethel, his maternal grandfather (fostered), or indicating the mixed backgrounds, if any, of his Geatish retainers (note that Hrothgar has warriors and officers with non-Danish backgrounds and that Beowulf's companion against the dragon, Wiglaf, is a Wægmunding not a Geat).

Why have they come? Obviously they lack permission to land but they would seek a different kind of permission: they would like the coast watch's willingness to have them seek his lord, the son of Healfdene, protector of the people ('leodgebyrgea' l. 269a). That last appellation indicates Beowulf's great respect for Hrothgar as a sitting king, despite the Grendel trouble. Moreover, Beowulf would seek the coast watch's lord out of a (reciprocally) loyal or true, retainer heart ('hold' – see D.H. Green on the reciprocal, ethical vocabulary of the warband).[5] Saying 'hold' is like saying his intended attitude toward Hrothgar is that of friend and loyal retainer all rolled together – no doubt an expression of intention and purpose the coast watch needs to hear. Beowulf certainly does not need the coast watch's martial opposition: he would win but then surely lose all possibility of undertaking the mission for which he has come. He urges the coast watch to be a good counsellor ('larena') to them (a friend who supports and teaches rather than one who commands). They are on a great and honourable mission to the lord of the Danes; nothing shall be secret. 'You know if it is true as we have heard that some sort of creature does secret, hateful deeds among the Scyldings in the dark of night. I might in noble spirit or mind advise Hrothgar how he, old and good, might overcome that enemy if to him a reversal ever should come, consolation for baleful affliction, for his whelming cares.' His motive phrase, 'rumne sefan,' l. 278a, will later have a near match when Hrothgar joyously calls him 'rumheort,' l. 1799, in the course of Beowulf 's magnanimous leave-taking on the morning after bringing Grendel's head and the giant sword hilt back to Heorot. But for now he is still partly unrevealed while wanting to face a terrible unknown. However, by putting the matter in terms of hearsay about terror – which the coast watch can confirm or not – and by focusing on Hrothgar's emotional suffering and the prospect of possible but not guaranteed reversal, Beowulf shows sensitivity as well as an awareness of contingency in his offer of noble advice for advice. The coast watch can accept this offer if he wants to. He has strongly fulfilled his part in confronting these strangers. He now needs to parse what the huge, splendidly equipped warrior among them has said and make the best of this situation – these men are heavily armed, notably led, and yet open-handed and willing to help in a dire matter the Danes have not solved for themselves. Still there is Danish pride and power to uphold, a need which will shift the scene's nuances from the direct, social world of an encounter to the nearly political.

Fearlessly, without hesitation ('unforht,' used also of what Grendel might do in the hall to Geats, that is, fearlessly eat them), the mounted official replies. He will not verbally score on the Geats now but he will withhold direct comment about their stated mission: 'Each (one of several) keen shield warrior shall know the difference between words and deeds, he who thinks well.' This opening maxim is neither quite answerable nor ignorable. It poses simultaneous possibilities: that the Geat leader speaks in terrible ignorance of the Grendel problem or else that he speaks falsely or else well. Events will tell. For himself, the coast watch has heard what he needed to hear: who the warriors are, who their leader's lord is, who their leader's father is, and especially, what this Geat war-band's ethical stance is toward Hrothgar. It is 'hold' toward the lord of the Scyldings – Beowulf's crucial term of reciprocal loyalty (l. 267a). Commenting on nothing else in Beowulf's speech, he continues to insist on his authority and the power of his presence when he imperatively tells them to go forth bearing their weapons and armour – 'I will guide you and likewise I will set a guard against enemies on your newly refitted ship, hold it in reciprocal

honour until it bears again the beloved men to the land of the Weder-
Geats, those who survive the rush of battle.'

He has been asked for advice: he gives it gnomically; then by way of
promised, personal escort (in this world 'counsel' is often a kind of
action, action a kind of counsel); and then by way of ambiguously
securing the new-tarred ship against any enemies ('wið feonda
gehwone,' l. 294a). This is of course militarily prudent as well as
helpful and indicates what he will allow: should the Geats survive the
rush of battle against Grendel, then they will leave. He will secure the
ship for that purpose as well as against any future treachery (should
the enemies in question prove to be the Geats themselves). He also
acknowledges who they are with a term politically more inclusive than
Beowulf's, thus indicating his sense of regions and the people in them.
As for Beowulf's characterization of Hrothgar's situation and emotions, he says nothing, while nevertheless acknowledging the force of
Beowulf's offer – battle – and indicating the likelihood that some Geats
will not survive the encounter even if all goes well.

On the journey to Heorot, the Geats, splendid and shining in their
boar helmets and armour, are a militarily impressive sight. We focus
on them as a promising group before the coast watch turns his horse,
points out the hall, and says it is time for him to return (to the coast).
Bidding that the all-ruling Father hold them in reciprocal honour ('ar')
and keep them safe in their venture, he blesses them in a sense, having
softened into social acceptance and implicit appreciation of these
'beloved' Geats (although beloved of whom is an ambiguity here) in
their professed mission.[6]

So, once again, the Geats arrive – this time by highway and to the
hall where another officer challenges them after the 'sea-weary' men
(an odd appellation here) stack their shields and spears against the hall
and sit on benches – as bold supplicants? They will again be con-
fronted, will through Beowulf exchange words, and will await word of
Hrothgar's initial decision. Then they will be shown in and Beowulf
will address Hrothgar directly. This series of arrivals is a complicated,
diplomatic pulse, after the varying, acceptable beats of which Beowulf
will be invited to sit and reveal his mind. But before moving to that
moment and Unferth's seemingly out-of-the-blue challenge, we need
to dwell on Wulfgar's. We need to pace these movements rather than
hurry through them.

'Whence come you carrying your gold plated shields, helmets and
war gear, your mass of spears?' Armed, they are a lively threat,

although they are sitting down, seem tired and thus are not in a potential attack posture; moreover he must know the coast watch has
escorted this troop toward Heorot and so his question is not one of surprise or present worry. Rather it is a demand for information about
origins, a demand softened somewhat by his following explanation
and enquiry: 'I am Hrothgar's honorable messenger and officer. Never
before have I seen so many brave, foreign men. I expect that you have
come in proud spirit, not at all as exiles or marauders ('nalles for
wræcsiðum, / ac for higeþrymmum Hrothgar sohton' [ll. 338b–339]);
rather, by naming the threat and dismissing it he suggests their best
motive: out of greatness of heart they have come to seek Hrothgar ('ac
for higeþrymmum,' l. 339a). Leadingly, he would give the Geats the
motives they must profess if they are to gain entry into Heorot.

Beowulf replies to Hrothgar's officer by first identifying the entire
war-band: 'we are Hygelac's table-companions; Beowulf is my name.
I would tell my mission or honorable message ('min ærende,' l. 345b)
to the son of Healfdene, famous prince, your chief, if he, the good one,
would grant that we might greet him.' They have come and would like
to present Beowulf and his mission to Hrothgar himself, who, while
famous in himself, is also the son of a fierce, glorious king (and thus
the living incarnation of a great, father-son pair). Beowulf's language
is more formal than I have indicated in its suspended clauses, as
though carefully weighed out, deliberative in its courting of permission: 'Would I say to the son of Healfdene, to the famous prince,
my mission, to the lord of yours, if he, to us will grant, that we him,
the good one, may greet.' Implicitly Beowulf interprets the officer's
demand as a request for war-band affiliation rather than for a place of
origin. He concedes his own name without knowing the officer's name
and then establishes his own importance by saying what he wants:
that his message is for Healfdene's son himself should that great king
vouchsafe him an audience. This puts Hrothgar's officer in his place
after a concession and involves three-part praise of Hrothgar himself
as well as the supposition that the famous prince might not see him
and hear what he has to say – a possibility Beowulf would have to
accept although he no doubt devoutly hopes otherwise. He does not
call his message a great one 'micel ærende' (l. 270b), as he does for the
coast watch's benefit, thus somewhat lowering his posture, that is, his
sense of the importance of what he has come to say and what he hopes
to do. This is diplomacy on his part in response to the officer's challenge. Moreover, as Andy Orchard has noted, his use of circumlocu-

tions for Hrothgar 'shows that he recognizes that his own mission is a delicate one.'[7]

In six lines Wulfgar – although still unidentified by name to Beowulf – elaborates upon Beowulf's honorifics for Hrothgar, calling Hrothgar the friendly lord of the Danes, distributor of rings, famous lord, the good or great one. This amplifies Hrothgar's prestige notably, independently of his father, as Wulfgar, apparently satisfied by Beowulf's identification of himself and his war-band, promises to ask Hrothgar, as Beowulf has petitioned, even stressing this point – that Beowulf is a petitioner. He will tell Hrothgar about Beowulf's coming, his voyage or mission, and he will speedily make known the answer that good or great one thinks to give.[8] He makes no promises, as though prestigious Hrothgar might in fact refuse an audience to Beowulf and the Geats. Practising good custom, Wulfgar goes then quickly to where Hrothgar sits, old and white-haired with his retinue of warriors. Upon reaching Hrothgar he stands by his shoulder and announces the arrival from afar of Geat warriors, the chief among them is called Beowulf. Their petitions are that they would in an exchange of words, 'wordum wrixlan,' speak with Hrothgar. He advises that Hrothgar not deny them his answer – implicitly, the shining, gracious Hrothgar should be gracious. For these Geats in their war gear seem worthy, he says, warriors to esteem; at any rate the leader is strong who has brought those warriors here. Implicitly it could be politically unwise not to grant their petition, either because they might react militarily to such a denial or else because they promise much in their appearance and being, especially in the body and person of their leader.

Hrothgar immediately acknowledges Beowulf, placing him in an indirect, social relationship to himself. He knew Beowulf as a boy, noting that Beowulf's father is Ecgtheow, to whom Hrethel of the Geats gave his daughter. Beowulf is the offspring of that marriage or alliance and has come here bravely seeking a reciprocally loyal, friendly lord: 'is his eafora nu / heard her cumen, sohte holdne wine' (ll. 375b–376). Hrothgar continues by informing Wulfgar that sailors who have brought gift-coins from us to the Geats – as an expression of our pleasure ('þyder to þance,' l. 379a) – say Beowulf has the strength of thirty men in his handgrip. 'God has sent him to us so that I might expect some change against Grendel's terror. I will give that good one treasures for his daring or might of mind ["modþræce"]. Be in haste to usher them in to see the kinship-band gathered together; also say that they are welcome [they are well-come and graciously invited] to the people of the Danes.' Here Hrothgar suggests if not a direct obligation on Beowulf's part at least a general, social, and political context of acceptable, established reciprocity. The Geats have already done something for the Danes; Hrothgar has in turn thanked them materially. Moreover, Beowulf's arrival – inherently threatening, destabilizing of face, potentially securing an obligation in turn – is attributed both to his (unexplained) *desire* to seek out a reciprocally friendly lord who knew his father and to divine favour. This uneasy combination of horizons, the personal and the divine, is something Hrothgar can accept, especially instrumentally and semi-reciprocally when linking divine favour to some expectation against Grendel's terror in the person of this enormously powerful offspring of a warrior for whom Hrothgar once settled a feud. In his desire for reversal against Grendel, Hrothgar leaps to heavenly bounds and has already assigned Beowulf as guardian against Grendel (at least prospectively).

Returning, Wulfgar says that his victory lord has commanded him to say that he knows their noble lineage and that they are to him (again) welcome here, you brave minded ones, from over the sea waves. Earlier, Wulfgar greatly expanded Hrothgar's importance through a string of appellations and here he has Hrothgar acknowledge the nobility of the Geats. The formality of this is a careful one. Moreover, the Geats are not welcomed loosely or as though they have no more social hurdles. Acknowledging their nobility, making them welcome – these only allow them into the hall and into Hrothgar's presence. Wulfgar then gives them permission to go in wearing their armour and helmets to gaze upon Hrothgar. They do not have to strip down to soft clothing – a concession that would in fact be humiliating. But they have to leave their shields and slaughter-spears to await the meeting or council of words. This too is a careful division of honour as well as prudent, although Beowulf probably would not have thought to come before the famous prince armed to the teeth. Presumably the Danes have their shields and spears close to hand, so that if the Geats, belying all appearances and expectations to the contrary, do prove to be marauders, the Danes might successfully defend themselves in a tight, spear-driven formation against even the enormous strength of Beowulf. Such a consideration, however, is not calculated here.

Beowulf then arises and proceeds with many of his warriors, prudently in turn leaving a few behind to guard the shields and spears. Beowulf moves into the hall until he stands at the hearth; there in his shining corselet he hails Hrothgar, wishing him well and identifying himself as Hygelac's kinsman and thane. He has now arrived in the hall and is standing in martial magnificence before Hrothgar, but he has not yet been invited to sit down and join the assembled, retainer kinship of the hall. His first move, after verbally saluting Hrothgar and wishing him luck, is to state his kinship and retainer allegiance to Hygelac (thus he both identifies himself and suggests that he has not come to find a lord, whatever desire it is that has moved him). He then boasts about his many glorious deeds in his earlier youth – implicitly a youth he has left behind (a point he makes explicit when replying about the Breca affair to Unferth later) – and says that the Grendel affair came to his attention in his country; sailors say that the best of halls stands idle and useless after evening light. Aware no doubt that in his great strength and relative youth, he embodies *celeritas* and thus might be prejudicially assessed as impetuous, given to magic and dangerous (see Sahlins on the young warrior's *celeritas* and the sitting king's *gravitas*, and below in chapter 3),[9] he says his own people, the best, wise men, urged him to seek Hrothgar because they knew his great strength. They have seen how he fought giants and in the waves slew water monsters at night, how he endured great distress in avenging Geat suffering or affliction, how he ground the monsters (who asked for it) to bits in his grasp. So now against Grendel, against that foe, he would alone hold a meeting, a Thing against the giant – relying on no magic aside from his crushing strength. This information contains leavening parts of boast, the establishment of credentials, of eye-witnessed but not painless triumphs on behalf of his people, and a proposal to meet alone, as though in violent but legal parlay, with Grendel ('ana gehegan / ðing wið þyrse,' ll. 425b–426a). Beowulf does not here predict a possible outcome, simply that he has, given his monster-slaying experience, hardened credentials worth considering in the Grendel affair.

Rounding out, he comes to his current request, what he would now have Hrothgar grant him, as though a favour of a singular kind ('anre bene,' l. 428b): now that he has come so far, please do not refuse his request that he alone with his warriors might purge Heorot. And as though this would seem overweening on his part, he says he will fight Grendel unarmed because he has heard that Grendel scorns weapons. This, he is sure, will please his lord, Hygelac, deeply. He will grapple with Grendel, foe against foe and hazard life; whomever death takes will abide God's judgment. This spectacular boast then modulates into acknowledgment that if Grendel manages to rule the battle hall he will unhesitatingly eat Geats just as he ate Danes in the past. This can happen. The Geats are not Grendel-proof any more than the Danes have been. Such a concession to this possibility adjusts Beowulf's vow and avoids insulting the Danes who have been helpless against Grendel. Should Grendel prevail, he says in a dark-humoured, eloquent way, there will be no need to cover his head for Grendel will already have done that. In word play, Beowulf says that if he dies Grendel will bear his bloody remains, by bolting them down, eating remorselessly, and thus mark his moor in gore. Hrothgar will not have to worry about Beowulf's corpse. But, should he die in battle, he would have his armour sent on to Hygelac. May events go as they will!

He has now twice reckoned his tie to Hygelac, suggesting that he thinks of himself only as a special, well-advised and legalistically minded petitioner (proposing a Thing with Grendel). Despite having initially responded to an ethical call – that Hrothgar has need of men – he is not a seeker of a new lord. He would please Hygelac in the way in which he chooses to fight, and, should he fail in the fight, he would have his perhaps semi-magical, heirloom armour – Weland's work, his maternal grandfather's corselet – returned to Hygelac (from whom it likely came as a fine acknowledgment of worth – thus a kind of indirect, material boast and validation). Having positioned himself as a foreign but entirely friendly, juridically balanced giant-fighter, he finishes not with a battle cry but with an acknowledgment of the fate that is unknowable beforehand. He now waits upon Hrothgar, who does not yet grant the desired petition. For how can he permit this to an as yet publicly untried foreign warrior among the Danes, no matter what conclusion he leapt to in his initial response to Wulfgar's address?

Socially face to face, he nevertheless must say something noncommittal yet encouraging and salving of his personal as well as Danish honour. This he begins to do by attributing motive and obligation on the friendly Beowulf's part as related to all Hrothgar once did in settling a feud on Beowulf's father's behalf (he does not attribute Beowulf's arrival in this face to face setting to divine agency). Thus he attributes Beowulf's arrival to generalized, almost free-floating marks of reciprocal honour in him ('for arstafum,' l. 458a). Hrothgar then indirectly warns Beowulf: meeting Grendel will not be a picnic; although God could easily prevent Grendel, and while it is grievous for him to tell anyone of this (Hrothgar suffers manfully), Grendel has swept away many of Hrothgar's warriors, those who boasted that they would stay in the hall and meet Grendel's battle with terrible swords;

but there in the morning the benches steamed with their gore and blood. He becomes personal, although his warriors' failures are not his: 'Then I had fewer, beloved warriors because of those whom death took.' In a sense, their failure took something from Hrothgar – their beloved, excellent selves – without any return or payment, something his honour requires and why finally he says *death* took them, rather than Grendel. Grendel has never offered compensation and certainly one cannot establish honourable reciprocities with death. So, with that grim impasse in mind, and having already heard a sample of Beowulf's brave eloquence, he tells Beowulf to sit and feast now, and in time, as he is moved, to disclose his thoughts as a victory-glorious man, or perhaps his thoughts of victory, as his mind whets him – a difficult passage perhaps because Hrothgar would have Beowulf truly show himself but not just in immediate response to Hrothgar's speech ('onsæl meoto ... swa þin sefa hwette,' ll. 489b–490b). An immediate response might not be trustworthy, whereas a disclosure as Beowulf is moved might be. In any case, we now have Beowulf's fourth arrival, in effect, coming in the course of feasting in Heorot. Having apparently passed this interview stage, and now fully in the hall and at table, Beowulf will be challenged further. Hrothgar's permission is still withheld, at least until Beowulf does something in public that shows his mettle.

Although he has already pronounced noble mindfulness in Beowulf, reminded us of ongoing reciprocity between Danes and Geats, and has now attributed Beowulf's arrival to an implicit, honouring obligation perhaps sprung from Hrothgar's aid and recruitment of Beowulf's father, Hrothgar can only entertain Beowulf's offer as something bravely proffered, not yet taken up, while hoping that Beowulf might have the mind he will need to go along with his great strength for the task at hand. Moreover, Hrothgar is the sitting king to whom gifts are brought and who distributes treasures and favours for the benefit and prosperity of all. Beowulf has more to prove before Hrothgar can grant his petition. We do not know what is coming until he who sits at Hrothgar's feet begins to speak in a direct, belittling challenge. If Beowulf does not do well against Unferth's sudden but permitted, even sanctioned, sally – for Unferth's challenge is very likely one of those events in time that Hrothgar anticipates will move or whet Beowulf – then Hrothgar would have no reason to think he will do well against Grendel's sudden terror. To give this Beowulf stewardship of the great hall likely would be to pollute it twice over – to entrust

Heorot to the unworthy, then suffer his slaughtered remains in the morning.

Notably, in this transitional moment, Wealhtheow does not appear with her mead cup. Instead an unnamed thane has a similar duty, as he bears in hand an ornamented ale-cup – just the kind of cup ('ealowæge') Hrothgar says Danish warriors once boasted over when they said they would stay and meet Grendel (l. 481); moreover, it is the kind of cup that later Beowulf will have Freawaru bear in the hall when he tells her story to Hygelac. How will Beowulf and the Geats fare? The cup reflects both social conviviality and is oath producing; still, past outcomes make the present moment ambiguous in its portent. Just here Unferth speaks out, unbinding his battle-runes.

Unferth is said to be 'displeased' by Beowulf's mission because he would not have any other man have more glory under the heavens than himself; he is said to envy such 'achievement,' the same word Beowulf uses when he asks to achieve something alone with Grendel – 'gehegan,' as though that particular request especially rankles Unferth. A similar displeasure is a prelude to feud renewed in the later Heathobard story Beowulf tells upon his return to Hygelac: there just as here it is in some understandable way provoked (there by Danes wearing the weapons of slain Heathobards; here by Beowulf's strong, even amazing boast, proposing as he does to meet Grendel unarmed, hoping to prevail where armed Danes have not). Although Unferth may be a sanctioned challenger, one of his offices then being to goad strangers into revealing themselves, the poet motivates him personally as well. Why? I suggest that just here Beowulf's posture as a foreign but entirely friendly, legalistically and ethically minded giant-slayer is in question. Could his real motive be glory, even vainglory as Unferth's always seems to be?

Unferth begins by suggesting there may be two Beowulfs: the pretender here in Heorot and the loser in the swimming contest with Breca, where foolishly life was risked in deep water. His eloquent speech invokes an utterly astonishing ambition attributed to Beowulf – that is, to measure the ocean path, to enfold it and weave it with his hands. Swimming for seven nights, Breca, in Unferth's version, overcame Beowulf, having the greater strength. Just so Unferth expects a worse outcome for Beowulf in the rush of battle, even though he has elsewhere triumphed, if he dares abide near Grendel the night long. Unferth does not question Beowulf's monster slaying credentials. Those events were witnessed by others. But he does accuse Beowulf of a foolhardy boast and of defeat in the swimming contest where Beowulf sought to weave the elements in the course of seeking victory. That failure is a harbinger of even greater failure here against the horribly 'elemental' Grendel should Beowulf dare await him. Group pride requires this challenge and this accusation. Now it is up to Beowulf to respond appropriately or not and thus reveal his turns of mind.

Beowulf attacks immediately, accusing Unferth of inflecting the story toward Breca's adventure (victory) because he has consumed a lot of beer. The truth is quite otherwise, and can be summarized thus: I possessed much greater sea-strength than any other man; moreover we were neophytes, young and, while we boasted about how we would swim out and risk our lives, those boasts were not hollow (implying that Unferth's are); we did as we said, carrying swords in our hands. Moreover, he adds, Breca did not out swim me; I swam alongside him. I would not leave him until a storm separated us after five days. Sea beasts dragged me down to the bottom and thought to banquet on me but I slew them (much as *you* think to banquet verbally on me, he seems to imply). After that, from the east light came, God's bright beacon (a sign of victory). Then, after slaying more sea creatures – events often save the unfated warrior, if his courage avails – the sea bore me to the land of Finns.

More than three times as long, Beowulf's reply to Unferth's challenge moves in waves, the first ending on a scathing maxim: perhaps Grendel is unbeatable but only the courageous can find out otherwise; then he closes on a crushing series of notes: 'that neither you nor Breca has done anything greater than I have with swords, although you have slain your brothers, for which you shall suffer in hell; moreover, Grendel would never have performed so many hateful deeds in Heorot if your courage and heart were as fierce in marshalled battle as you yourself maintain; instead he has discovered that he need not dread feud from your people, the Victory-Scyldings; instead he spares none of the people of the Danes.' This apparent insult takes in all of the Danes, emphasizing irony in the traditional epithet. However, it grows directly out of Beowulf's address to Unferth and is in fact contingent on that attack, as though Unferth suddenly has personally become leader of the Danes ('eower leode'). Beowulf's scorning of Unferth falls, because of him, on all the Danes for the moment. Then Beowulf shifts perspective and brutally states the Danes' plight at Grendel's hands: he takes his exactions, sparing none as he carries away his pleasure, killing and feasting. But I will show him the valour and might of the Geats in battle, soon, now ('ungeara nu,' l. 602b).' There will be no putting off, no delay (a further insult). In the morning light whoever may can go to the meadhall in high spirits; the radiantly clothed sun will shine from the south – imagery that supposes glorious victory, although Beowulf does not flatly predict that he will prevail.

Unferth does not reply. But Hrothgar is now confident that he can count on Beowulf for help of the sort that Beowulf will again promise when he takes his leave of Hrothgar three days later, when he would return to Hygelac ('geoce'). While Beowulf does not seem to have calculated the impression he might make on Hrothgar – aside from his reference in passing to the many terrors Grendel has performed against Unferth's lord ('gryra gefremede, / ... ealdre þinum,' ll. 591b–592b) – what Hrothgar has heard of Beowulf's firm, utterly resolute thought ('fæstrædne geþoht,' l. 610b) has convinced the shepherd of the people, the distributor of treasure. This Beowulf, this exceptionally powerful warrior, goes in mind and body for the jugular. Hrothgar's countenance probably encourages an upsurge in the hall of warrior laughter, pleasing shouts, and delighted words, all of which is a sort of hurrah for Beowulf's finish and his battle-resolve.

Notable for both its social and political moment, just at this point Wealhtheow emerges, moving forth in a regal progress around the hall. Gold-adorned, bearing the mead-filled 'ful,' Wealhtheow eventually in her circuit comes to Beowulf and thanks God that she can trust in a warrior for solace or relief against crime. Her trust here is exactly Hrothgar's as well – 'gelyfan.' Beowulf partakes ('geþicean') of the 'ful' from Wealhtheow, this fierce warrior (slaughterer – 'wælreow,' l. 629) ready for battle: he then speaks to her, saying what he resolved to do when still at sea – that he 'by all means with his war band would work the will of your people or else die in the slaughter, firmly held in the fiend's grasp,' ending with a resounding vow. 'I will accomplish a manly deed of valour or abide the end of my days in this meadhall.' That report of his resolve while at sea cannot be precisely accurate, for he has yet to know Wealhtheow. By putting his resolve as he does – addressing her in the possessive pronoun – Beowulf responds to her cup offering directly and for the moment exclusively. The Danes are her people and he has committed himself to working their will, which then is hers as well. His concluding vow shows his continuing resolve, after all he has heard about Grendel's savagery, and suggests that he has no ambition but to serve in this matter to the death, if that is how it turns out. His words please Wealhtheow, who moves then to complete her circuit and sit again next to her lord, Hrothgar, she, this gold-adorned, excellent queen of the people. High ritual permeates the scene.

Before Unferth's challenge, there is no Wealhtheow present and the drinking is from an ale-cup – sociable and welcoming, although one can drink too much and become loose-tongued, as Beowulf has charged Unferth with being. Wealhtheow's emergence bearing the 'ful' is both regal and somehow sacral; partaking of it is then like a sacrament – one is confirmed as an intimate member of the group and what one says is sacred oath. This is more than 'peace-weaving,' a term that does not come up in the scene. Wealhtheow is more like the regal maker of a covenant through the sharing of the 'ful,' committing all to each other and drawing Beowulf's deepest resolve out into public statement – his mind now fully revealed; his powerful person fully committed. Helen Damico, besides perceptively arguing for Wealhtheow's essential strength of character and presence in Heorot, has convincingly expressed this 'ful' bearing role of hers in relation to 'a pagan ritual described in the heroic lays and the sagas. The *bragarfull* "cup, or toast, of the king". At this ceremony, a hero (or heroes) makes an oath (the *heitstrenging* "solemn vow"), too sacred to be broken under any circumstances, while drinking from the *bragarfull*.'[10] Moreover, following Francis P. Magoun, Helen Damico suggests that Wealhtheow in her ring-adorned person may have a quasi-priestess function in the hall – perhaps of Freya or as her surrogate.[11] Charlotte Behr might concur given her study of the Scandinavian context for, and the Odin-based origin myths behind, the all-gold bracteates found in high-status female graves.[12] So we have gone from an ascending series of warrior arrivals to regal procession, coming and going around the hall, and drink-solemn ritual.

Hrothgar can now, as he will, entrust the hall to Beowulf's special hands and to his enormously strong stewardship. The great, sitting king has attracted and fully accepted the awesome, fierce warrior prince he needs – a prince who in turn has consistently spoken his ethical and honourable intentions toward Hrothgar as well as his sacred vow now to do the will of Wealhtheow's people – not his own in any self-serving way – or die in the hall (perhaps Beowulf especially respects queens, bringing gifts as he does to Hygd in his eventual homecoming). At some point during the ensuing festivities Wealhtheow leaves the hall to Hrothgar and his warriors and so also to

Beowulf and his men. This sets up a carefully paced, face-to-face inter-action between Hrothgar and Beowulf, great king and hugely promis-ing warrior. Wealhtheow's key, queenly mission has been accom-plished: to solicit and receive Beowulf's final, deep, conclusive vow.[13] She can now leave the men to their gestures of turning over and receiv-ing possession of the hall, which, after all, Hrothgar commanded and named.

In that face-to-face encounter, before Hrothgar departs for the night, leaving Beowulf and the Geats to their test against Grendel, whom Hrothgar knows will come – a grim knowledge that conditions his prudence – we have a significant, often hastily treated passage:[14]

> Gegrette þa   guma oþerne,
> Hroðgar Beowulf,   ond him hæl abead,
> winærnes geweald,   ond þæt word acwæð:
> 'Næfre ic ænegum men   ær alyfde,
> siþðan ic hond ond rond   hebban mihte,
> ðryþærn Dena   buton þe nu ða.
> Hafa nu ond geheald   husa selest,
> gemyne mærþo,   mægenellen cyð,
> waca wið wraþum!   Ne bið þe wilna gad,
> gif þu þæt ellenweorc   alder gedigest.'
> Ða him Hroþgar gewat   mid his hæleþa gedryht,
> eodur Scyldinga   ut of healle;
> wolde wigfruma   Wealhþeo secan,
> cwen to gebeddan.   Hæfde Kyningwuldor
> Grendle togeanes,   swa guman gefrungon,
> seleweard aseted;   sundornytte beheold
> ymb aldor Dena,   eotonweard' abead.   (ll. 652–68)

Much is packed into these lines and into Hrothgar's seven-line speech, in the opening course of which Hrothgar, ruler of the meadhall, for-mally greets Beowulf (as Beowulf greets Hrothgar, so that this is a mutual address and greeting, a reciprocal, thus face to face exchange) and wishes him luck ('hæl' here being related to good omen, as Geat wisemen foresaw) before turning Heorot over to Beowulf and the Geats. After doing so, Hrothgar leaves the hall and seeks his queen, having set a hall guard against Grendel. This seemingly simple sequence of actions is socially quite complicated and formal. Poten-tially fraught with difficulty, even peril, and not just for Beowulf and his men, this passage has in subtle ways escaped most readers and translators.

Foremost, Hrothgar's action is a highly formal bestowing of the hall unto Beowulf, who, in receiving and defending it, will perform a special service for Hrothgar, a 'sundornyt,' as he offers an anti-giant guardianship against Grendel ('eotonweard abead,' l. 668b). But in allowing Beowulf to occupy the hall as its first surrogate guardian and holder against terror, a point Hrothgar emphasizes, he still acts as the superior giver and conferrer of privilege. There is no irony in his departure, the protector of the Scyldings with his troop of warriors, as he, the battle chief ('wigfruma,' l. 664a), seeks Wealhtheow. Indeed, there is something shining and grand, even splendid in his power and his Scylding procession out of the hall, as there will be in his re-entry, a form of reinvestiture, the next morning – according to P.B. Taylor.[15] But how to suggest the extent of what is going on here in this depar-ture at the end of Beowulf's sequence of arrivals? How do we render the social nuances such that we do not read Hrothgar's speech and the poet's narrative movement as ironic at Hrothgar's expense and as sug-gesting Hrothgar's martial weakness (which in fact is only the case in this horrible affair with Grendel, charmed against weapons)? More-over, how can we understand Hrothgar's departure to seek his queen as anything other than a retreat suggesting the overwhelming terror soon to come?

First of all, we have to be careful. We have to ask social and cultural questions that may not come immediately to mind from within the habitual, social ways in which we think. For instance, when someone invites us into her home and hands it over to us, with the keys, we read no special social significance into that act other than friendship or, at least, trust (assuming that the homeowner in question cares for his or her home). We are not given the home for the night in any special sense. At most we might think of ourselves as something between house-sitters and trusted stewards. If in addition we are expected to defend the home against an anticipated, violent break-in, we might think of ourselves as vigilantes and the home in question as merely a site of defence. We would not readily suppose that we were perform-ing a special function in an almost hallowed hall as the surrogate power of a great battle king. But just that is essentially what Beowulf is invited to do and what he does.

If we say that Hrothgar simply leaves the hall to seek his consort's bed, the almost pre-emptory character of this action fails to convey the sense of rhythm, of progression, probably of procession carried by the half-line by half-line syntax of the original. Similarly, Hrothgar has done something highly legislative in a sense when temporarily conferring the hall into Beowulf's keeping on his behalf, that is, permitting or granting this keeping – an action only a few readers have noted as especially formal. David Day in his dissertation on 'Jurisdiction and Justice in Beowulf' considers Hrothgar's gestures as formally conveying Hrothgar's *mund* or possession of the hall over to Beowulf.[16] Also prominently among those few are John Josias Conybeare early in the nineteenth century and Ruth Lehman in the twentieth.[17]

Lehman translates the line into a long one of permission: 'Now you may have and hold this house of splendor.' Conybeare, while not translating the passage, says that Hrothgar retires to his chamber after 'having previously saluted Beowulf, and committed to him in form the charge and defence of his palace for the night.'[18] That Hrothgar has done so, along with a temporary transference of his royal 'mund' to Beowulf, if that is what he does – these moves should cause us to re-examine the compound 'kyningwuldor,' which Klaeber makes into a term for God. The 'king of glory' in l. 665b could well be Hrothgar himself, certainly a 'glory-king' if we avoid the partitive Klaeber hears in the compound. Hrothgar prominently leaves Heorot, going out of the hall to seek Wealhtheow, his queen, in their bedchamber. But the evoking of Hrothgar's exalted status does not end there, on what for us has often seemed an oddly connubial, anticlimactic and thus ironic note. For the king has done what he has done royally, just as he, as glory-king, has royally set or toweringly established someone against Grendel (the word for 'setting' appearing elsewhere in the poem only where Danes set golden banners for Scyld's funeral ship).

Beowulf is now the legal, rightful holder and defender of the hall against Grendel, a special office ('sundornyt') Beowulf will perform on behalf of the lord of the Danes. Thus Hrothgar's prominence in the passage, beginning with his greeting of Beowulf in line 653, continues to the end, line 668. Then the poet turns to Beowulf and to the reliance Beowulf has on his great strength, the Ruler's favour.

Even here a certain formality characterizes what Beowulf says and does as he anticipates the arrival of his dishonorable guest: he removes his helmet, gives his decorated, ornamented sword – which may have been Ongentheow's sword, taken from the slain king and given to Hygelac (l. 2988) – to the safe keeping of a trusted, warrior-steward ('ombihtþegn'). Before he steps up to the bed where he will await

Grendel's entry into the hall, he speaks formally to his retainers, saying that he does not consider his battle-swelling, his martial work more poorly than Grendel does his. Because Grendel fights unarmed so will Beowulf (adversarial courtesy toward his anticipated guest). Grendel, Beowulf avers, does not know that good practice of cutting a shield to pieces, strong though he is in his dire, malicious work.

If Grendel dares seek battle without weapons, or is above the use of weapons (Beowulf does not know that Grendel is charmed against weapons), he and Beowulf will tonight put aside the sword. Let the wise God, the holy Lord assign glory on either hand as He thinks most meet. Far from being merely boastful or arrogant or just lucky in his boast, this courtesy and balance toward his adversary's approach and way of fighting is exemplary; Beowulf's deference toward divine decision is the same, although he is wrong in thinking that he could easily kill Grendel with a sword (as he some time ago slew sea monsters after the swimming contest with Breca). His retainers, having along with Beowulf heard all that Grendel has done, fear they will not survive the night, that they will never see their beloved homeland again. In this only one is prophetically right: he will be snatched out of his sleep and devoured. The rest awaken during the encounter and draw their swords to help Beowulf, whose knowledge of Grendel's deeds has only steeled him in his martial courtesies.[19]

But to return to the point when Hrothgar has yet to leave the hall, we need to keep as fully in mind as possible the social situation here, especially the reciprocal values expressed in and through that situation, which include a sense of great promise in Hrothgar's stately departure and his setting of a special hall guard. Various items of diction as well as the measured progress of the verse itself demand our attention, needing some kind of approximate rendering perhaps even at the expense of modern fluency and directness. We need not return to Francis Gummere's bouncing and now quaint 'have now and hold this house unpeered; remember thy glory; thy might declare.' But, and here is the surprise given how much one wants verse translations of the poem, perhaps something more like R.K. Gordon's 1926 rendition should inspire us: '"Have now and hold the best of houses. Be mindful of fame, show a mighty courage, watch against foes. Nor shalt thou lack what thou desirest, if with thy life thou comest out from that heroic task." Then Hrothgar went his way with his band of heroes, the protector of Scyldings out of the hall; the warlike king was minded to seek Wealtheow the queen for his bedfellow. The glorious king had, as men learned, set a hall guardian against Grendel. He performed a special task for the prince of the Danes, kept watch against the giant.'[20]

Gordon achieves a formal, even old-fashioned quality here. In a different context, as a warning against what he calls false colloquialism and modernity, J.R.R. Tolkien wants to acknowledge the poem's archaic vocabulary, and word order, 'artificially maintained as an elevated and literary language.'[21] Possibly one can make a case for keener effort of that sort, perhaps even for a biblical style (as in 'smite,' not 'whack'). Tolkien reminds us that 'the development of a form of language familiar in meaning and yet freed from trivial associations, and filled with the memory of good and evil, is an achievement, and its possessors are richer than those who have no such tradition.'[22] Perhaps, then, for both semantic and cultural accuracy, we should prefer prose in our translations, opening up room for connotatively rich renderings of words into phrases and lines into the progressions of suspension and variation, of complicated syntax. In doing that we can gain expressive access at the syntactical and even morphological level to the poem's rhythms inside its larger, narrative pulses, to which we should now return.

To summarize, Beowulf has been granted a special guardianship, unlike any Hrothgar has given before. He has arrived now at his immediate goal – to meet and greet Grendel fiercely, because Hrothgar has need of this and Grendel has for too long been a criminal curse. Beowulf disarms himself and speaks to his anxious men (whose courage is not at his level, although they willingly abide with him and keep their swords handy) and he defers to God as the assigner of glory. The dramatic action then closes on those lines of deference while the poet assures us that no matter what the less than confident Geats think – Beowulf aside – God will weave good speed in war for them, He who has always ruled mankind. Just here we would expect a significant stop – perhaps even a break the scribe could mark with a new fit. But after the poet's sententious remark about God, the verb 'com' follows immediately, bringing night and the shadow-walker directly into the extended moment. The effect is like a doubled or skipping pulse – stuttering from an assertion of God's dominion directly into an expression of Grendel's coming in the dark.

When the victory becomes Beowulf's and the Geats', a significant social problem arises for Hrothgar and the Danes: how to incorporate this hoped for but by no means guaranteed victory on their behalf by outsiders, who, while clearly established as special guardians in one's hall, have nevertheless done something one could not do for oneself. Gratitude, no matter how immense, rests uneasily, at least initially, on a surface of tender pride and vulnerable honour. Both the poet and Hrothgar have to work through this problem.

CHAPTER THREE

The Arrival of Joy after Grendel's Departure, and a Momentous Question: Succession or Not?

From the moment he returns to Heorot on the morning after Grendel's defeat, Hrothgar, while committed to rewarding Beowulf handsomely – 'Ne biþ þe wilna gad, / gif þu þæt ellenweorc aldre gedigest' (ll. 660b–661), moves both regally and aggressively. He seizes the social moment by tring to increase and indeed exploit the promise of this glorious scene in which many come to see Grendel's arm and shoulder.[1] Hrothgar comes from his queen's apartment or chamber, the ring hoard's lord, having walked or stepped (a stately progress, no doubt) 'firm in glory' ('tryddode tirfæst,' l. 922a). That phrase about glory strikes some people as ironic; however, it is apt because Hrothgar has the glory of his own past, his great line of kings and two-generational kingships and now Beowulf's victory over Grendel, Hrothgar having set Beowulf as hall guard for the night. What he is prepared to do now is offer adoption and some kind of right of succession to Beowulf, this by way of the great gifts he will bestow on the son of a renowned warrior he recruited long ago. The nature of those gifts speaks volumes as they mark a highly forward, even aggressive, move on Hrothgar's part.[2]

True, as Mary Dockray-Miller has nicely observed about the Grendel fight, Hrothgar loses masculinity on martial grounds in comparison to the hyper-masculine Beowulf[3] – but battle is not the only arena for winning and losing masculinity and thus honour. One can win or lose in the hall as well, as Unferth clearly has in Beowulf's crushing finish to his account of the Breca episode – a point returned to when Breca further loses some honor in comparison to Beowulf's willingness to seek Grendel's mother. But honour can potentially be won or lost to some extent in any exchange between men – as happens both positively and negatively for Unferth in the course of loaning Hrunting to Beowulf. Both possession of the famous sword and that gesture itself are honour enhancing; here Unferth, who does not allude again to the Breca episode, is said to be strongly knit, powerful ('eafoþes cræftig,' l. 1466a).

That point is often lost in the vast literature about Hrothgar as a weak king when compared to the active hero. Scott DeGregorio surveys the relevant scholarship in anticipation of his view that the honorific epithets applied to Hrothgar are not univalent in their narrative contexts. Instead they exist 'within a field of possibilities whose parameters are defined by the frictions within and interrelations between the various perspectives at stake'[4] – such as, for example, how wise is Hrothgar to try to settle the feud between Danes and Heathobards by marrying his daughter to Ingeld, and why does he have Unferth and Hrothulf prominent in his court rather than the battle-staunch Æschere? Those questions are unanswerable and depend in part on arguable views of Unferth as unaccountably nasty and Hrothulf at least as a future traitor to Hrothgar's sons. What is notable here, however, is DeGregorio's sense of friction within the various perspectives through which Hrothgar appears to us – the major one, for this section, being his remarkable role as an established 'sitting' king famous in his prestige and active in the hall.

Hrothgar comes to the hall with a great company, the very best of their class ('cystum gecyþed,' l. 923a), and his queen also. Both measure (*metan*) or traverse the path to the meadhall with troops of attendants. These are highly formal, regal progressions, with lord and queen possibly emerging separately from their apartment although close together and respectively attended. In such movement alone Hrothgar and his queen assert their exalted, regal status and power. His is the masculinity here of royal progress, presence, and voice. Using a distinction taken from Georges Dumézil's analysis of Indo-European kingship, Marshall Sahlins introduces *celeritas* and *gravitas* into his discussion of Fijian kingship.[5] In those terms Hrothgar, who will of course speak first and act, reflects mainly *gravitas* whereas the vigorous, immensely strong Beowulf reflects the triumph of *celeritas*. The latter 'refers to the youthful, active, disorderly, magical, and creative violence of conquering princes; *gravitas*, to the venerable, staid, judicious, priestly, peaceful, and productive dispositions of an established people.' Sahlins adds that the 'combination of two terms produces a third, a sovereign power, itself a dual combination of the war function and the peace function, king and priest, will and law.' 'But the same creative violence that institutes society [as in Scyld Scefing's case by establishing boundaries with the sword] would be dangerously unfit to constitute it [toward which Scyld moves when he establishes tribute relationships]. The combination of the terms produces a third ... In fact, the warrior functions of the ruling chief dissolve as soon as possible on a youthful heir [the situation in *Beowulf* differing ideally in that a vigourous father is still wanted] ... Or else *gravitas* and *celeritas* are divided between junior and senior lines [as perhaps with brothers in *Beowulf*] or reigns might alternate.' But however organized within cohorts or across two generations, 'this [dual] determination of the sovereignty is an ambiguity that is never resolved.'[6]

Emphasizing that ambiguity is a far better way dynamically to understand kingship (as in the Danish myth of kingship sketched in chapter 1) and virtuous duality in *Beowulf* than is the older, more static notion, made famous by Robert Kaske, of fortitude and sapience,[7] both terms of which carry unwanted implications, such as in the one case stoicism, firmness, forbearance, and endurance (a strand quite alien to energetic action in the poem); whereas in the other, in matters of sapience, prudence and policy ought to prevail (although prudence is relevant in Hrothgar's mind, what is wise to do in the poem's world, such as avenging the death of a friend, often has little to do with Roman ideas of policy). Moreover, neither term entails vigorous, violent energy or productive power (there is rarely anything like physical strength in classical *fortitudo*); and either term might in Kaske's rendering exclusively constitute the virtue of a king – the combination as an ideal notwithstanding. Finally, kingship as a dynamic institution modelled across two generations is not considered here.

Thus for Kaske, Hygelac is all fortitude, despite the poet's characterization of him as, albeit hardy in battle, also reciprocally loyal, even joyful in his mutual relationship with his nephew ('Hygelac wæs / niða heardum nefa swyðe hold, / ond gehwæðer oðrum hroþra gemyndig,' ll. 2169b–2171). Moreover, Beowulf also attributes kindness and joy to him (l. 2150) and the poet thinks of Hygelac as the more illustrious of the two (l. 2199b). For his part, Hygelac piously thanks God that he can see Beowulf safe and sound (l. 1997b). Turning to Hrothgar, Kaske constructs an interesting disability: his weakened *fortitudo* negatively affects his powers of judgment, his *sapientia*, which is why he tolerates Hrothulf and follows apparently bad advice in marrying Freawaru to Ingeld. In the first case, the point is moot if we do not read treacherous irony into the relationship; and on the second point Hrothgar's wise advisers convince him to try and settle the feud through a marriage alliance. How unwise is one to heed wisdom, even if one cannot control for possible, undesirable outcomes? So, whatever merit Kaske's terms have they are applied oddly and are deeply alien to the nature of the world and the characters we see in the poem.

Rather than parcel out one or another virtue to individual kings, we do better to consider that all Beowulfian kings embody the combination Sahlins speaks of; Hrothgar swings to the *gravitas* side in his long rule and Beowulf retains the great war power of the young prince, *celeritas*, although he wonders how to focus that power nakedly against the dragon. This combination makes for ambiguity to varying degrees in any kingship, especially in any sequence of kings. Hrothgar's predecessors, beginning with Scyld Scefing, were more or less highly aggressive kings who terrorized their neighbours and who enjoyed martially worthy offspring – thus fulfilling the two-generational model given in chapter 1. Hrothgar in himself combines both in his early incarnation and then, after Grendel disables the hall at night, he suddenly becomes the 'sitting' king to whom things are brought first (ceremonially, as with the meadcup, and later properly as with Grendel's head and the giant, rune-inscribed sword hilt). His chief functions then are to receive, share out and legislate in what he proposes, pronounces and how he disposes. It is in those terms that Hrothgar maintains pre-eminence, expressing an active, honorable masculinity in the hall.

The poet passes over Hrothgar's actual arrival and disposition of himself and the great company of choice warriors. Hrothgar speaks, 'he who to the hall went, stood on the steps, saw the high roof, gold adorned and Grendel's hand.' Here Hrothgar is what he does and says in measured sequences. For this sight of Grendel's hand he thanks the All-Ruler, noting that he himself has suffered much that was hateful, injury by Grendel. But God may work 'wonder after wonder' (as though God indeed has brought this trophy to him). Speaking in the first person, he adds that not long ago he thought he would never experience reversal for the bloody suffering, compensation for the best of halls standing drenched in gore. Even this sorrowful thought indicates his power – *he* did not think that *he* would see a reversal, compensation for those bloody times. But now, he says, a warrior has 'through the Lord's might performed a deed' the Danes could not in 'their wisdom accomplish' – we all could not, he says. Their failure is collective but the slaughter in Heorot has been his grief alone, he seems to imply; and now through God's might a warrior has done what he and the Danes could not (the reference to God's power partially extenuates Danish failures). When Hrothgar turns to Beowulf, we can ask what he wants of this great warrior. What does he need? What must he do? In the course of several exchanges with Beowulf between now and Beowulf's eventual departure home, Hrothgar's direct addresses reflect his shifting wants and needs – to which Beowulf is curiously inattentive if we look for a direct reply. However, it is in this extended context of Hrothgar's repeated gestures and *changing* offers that we can best understand Beowulf's offer of military assistance in his eventual leave-taking from Hrothgar and Hrothgar's answering pronouncement, made in love and backed by his own great power, of continuing reciprocity between Danes and Geats. That pronouncement is the culmination of his expressions of masculinity in the hall.

Initially, without asking, Hrothgar simply declares: 'Now I, Beowulf, *you* [emphasis mine], the best of warriors, to me as a son will love in mind and heart ('freogan on ferhþe,' l. 948a, a powerful, emotion-laden phrase used only once elsewhere when the Geats mourn Beowulf's death). He formally enjoins Beowulf: 'Hold forth well this new kinship'; Beowulf will 'lack for nothing of worldly goods or desires' that Hrothgar has the power to wield or control ('þe ic geweald hæbbe,' l. 950b). This is an amazingly strong gesture and set of statements. It is a sweeping offer of adoption in relation to a non-verbal but no less overt offer of a leading place in the Danish line of succession – the latter conveyed clearly to everyone in the hall by the dynastic nature and functional history (Hrothgar's personal war gear) of the great treasures Hrothgar gives Beowulf.[8] Hrothgar must reward Beowulf; Hrothgar wants to recruit Beowulf, and so his actions can express several things simultaneously. Hrothgar needs some assurance that after his death the Danes will not be leaderless and vulnerable. More, he may need to repair the weakened model of kingship that Grendel's raids in effect devolved upon him. After all, Hrothgar's sons are young; neither can take on martial activities while Hrothgar still lives, and, further, he has outlived his vigorous brothers. Whatever ties he has to martial Swedes through the marriage of his sister to Onela are never alluded to and thus not counted on. How better, then, to secure some assurance about the future, and refresh the dual nature of kingship, than to bind this God-blest warrior to himself through adoption and dynastic recruitment?

In his reply to the adoption speech Beowulf emphasizes his reciprocal 'favouring' ('estum miclum') as the spirit in which he performed (having before the Grendel fight indicated his enduring tie to Hygelac by urging Hrothgar to send his armour to Hygelac should death take him). Acting in that spirit, Beowulf honours Hrothgar in return. But there is an asymmetry in this relationship and so Beowulf goes on to apologize in effect for a partial failure, for not being able to kill Grendel in the hall where Hrothgar could see the monster for himself. Still, although Grendel pulled away, he left his hand behind and fled, no doubt now 'narrowly bound in evil bonds' as he awaits 'the glorious Measurer's great judgment' (ll. 976b–977a; 978b–979a). The sign of victory is clear and the eventual judgment of deity is on our side, Beowulf seems to say. While honouring Hrothgar and no doubt noting Hrothgar's language, Beowulf seems to look above Hrothgar's pre-emptory adoption. The poet helps him here, in effect, by turning to the sight of Grendel's huge hand with its steel-like nails before narrating the refurbishing of Heorot for a celebratory banquet. In the early course of that banquet, where much amity is expressed between friends (Hrothgar and Hrothulf especially), Healfdene's son gives Beowulf the great gifts Beowulf will later in turn render up to Hygelac, his lord and uncle. Beowulf is urged to use them well – a highly ritualistic injunction – which carries an invitation, I would say ('het hine wel brucan,' l. 1045b, accords with the prior injunction to hold well the new kinship Hrothgar has decreed – 'heald forð tela / niwe sibbe' ll. 948b–949a). In the order of bestowal, Beowulf has just received Hrothgar's war saddle and Hrothgar has been denominated as protector of the 'friends of Ing,' perhaps a god-sprung appellation.[9] The whole divine and martial aura of Danish kingship as invested in Hrothgar is here invoked and posed as a question: will Beowulf in accepting the gifts take up a leading place in that line? Moreover, if he does, Hrothgar will not only have succeeded in recruiting in turn this great son of Ecgtheow's; he will have done what is possible to repair the Danish myth of kingship, passing on to a stupendous successor, while he the king still lives, his role as martial king. In such a move, by repairing a broken model of king-ship and succession, Hrothgar would culturally parallel Beowulf's purgation of the hall.

Wealhtheow, who has been in the background until now, perhaps with her many attendants, steps forth after we hear the Finn digres-sion and forcefully and materially counters Hrothgar's offer of the succession. In speaking directly to Hrothgar she first diplomatically presents him with the meadcup, calling him her lord and distributor of treasure. She further urges the right behaviour of speaking in 'gen-erous words' with the Geats and being kind toward them. However, now she moves to her main topic: less diplomatically and conceding less, although not insultingly, she says she has 'heard' that Hrothgar would adopt Beowulf, yet 'Heorot is cleansed.' Tom Shippey notes her 'implicature,' that Beowulf is no longer needed.[10] She would rather insist that Hrothgar honour Beowulf of course, but continue to enjoy his many treasures and goods; and when he does move on out of this life, he should leave his kingdom to his sons. She says she knows her gracious Hrothulf ('Ic mine can / glædne Hroþulf,' ll. 1180b–1181a), who, because suitably reminded of his debts to Hroth-gar and Wealhtheow, will no doubt serve as protector of their young sons (most readers register dramatic irony in this, thinking of Hrothulf as an eventual usurper of the line of succession – a reading that is arguable). She then approaches Beowulf with counter gifts, addressing him as he sits *between* her two sons (one assumes Hroth-gar has invited him to sit there as an expression of the new kinship he offers). Beowulf has not responded to Hrothgar's gifts other than to receive them and to accept the *ful* (a ceremonial cup filled with mead), thus drinking to the amity and honour of the moment. But his place on a bench next to the young princes indicates the seriousness of Hrothgar's gestures, as does their public nature, especially concern-ing the four great gifts – a golden banner, a helmet and mailshirt, a famous, bejewelled sword – of which the poet says in a suggestive formula that he has 'never heard' of four such gold-adorned gifts given in a more *friendly* fashion (emphasis mine, l. 1027) – a great king's friendliness having to do more with protection and honour, with sovereign smiling upon, than is our idea of friendship or inti-mate sharing.

Beowulf also drinks to what in effect is Wealhtheow's counter-giving, whereby she would counter or compete with Hrothgar's adoption gestures. Implicitly he acknowledges her desire that he treat her sons with mainly kindred-kind feeling, her vocabulary coming from the world of family ties and advice rather than retainer ties ('lara liðe,' l. 1220a); she would not have him become their lord and protector. She also enjoins Beowulf, urging him: 'Bruc ðisses beages, Beowulf leofa, / hyse, mid hæle' (ll. 1216–1217a). 'Beloved Beowulf, young warrior, use these gifts in prosperity and luck.' She will reward him for his kind behaviour. Beowulf accepts drinks from the *ful* before her giving and accepts the gifts and her injunctions wordlessly. The silent question now arises: will Beowulf eventually act on Hrothgar's wishes or will he accept the role Wealtheow would have him play in relation to her sons and to herself? Grendel's mother comes later that night, and so we lack an answer to this question the morning after. Instead Hrothgar now has an immediately pressing wish, a need momentarily more acute than any want he has revealed up to this point – redress for the loss of his shoulder companion and counsellor, Æschere (Grendel's mother having taken him along with Grendel's trophy arm).

When Beowulf arrives before dawn with his battle-troop, he first politely enquires if Hrothgar has spent a pleasant night. This innocent question, in the circumstances, could have ironic and insulting tones – a possibility registered in Hrothgar's abrupt negative: 'Do not you ask about joy,' continuing in a mixture of lament and near accusation. 'Sorrow is renewed; Dead is Æschere, Yrmenlaf's elder brother, my counsellor and shoulder-companion. A monster she has avenged the feud in which you yesterday night killed Grendel.' As Shippey notes, 'characters in heroic societies are prickly: stiff, on their dignity, ready to take offence, therefore requiring careful handling.'[11] Beowulf has literally walked into this one, his arrival and greeting surprised by Hrothgar's bitter news. But he need not backpedal, for Hrothgar will soon strongly imply a line of help on Beowulf's part, such that Beowulf's opening moment can pass into oblivion. Before he does that, however, he characterizes the Grendel terrain as weird, forbidding; he notes wolf-cliffs, high crags, dangerous paths; also a rushing stream that falls down the mountain, disappearing under the rocks. All of this only a mile or so from Heorot; over it – the mere – hang frost-covered trees and there is fire in the seemingly bottomless water at night: 'that is not a pleasant place!' Animals fear it; even a hunted stag will turn back toward its pursuers rather than plunge into that lake.

Why Hrothgar would so creepily characterize the monsters' mere is an interesting question. After all, after Beowulf's purgation of Heorot the day before, excited Danes raced their horses to the edge of the mere, following Grendel's bloody tracks. The way was easy and the mere-side unforbidding. Perhaps Hrothgar's mere, now in the loss of Æschere, is psychologically a different place – or at least the mere has a mixed geography. In any case, Hrothgar gives Beowulf ample room to wiggle if he wants to, for no man is wise enough to know the depths of that place. Better still, he would motivate Beowulf, challenge him by the fearsomeness of the prospective task (the female did start, as it were, when men drew swords; so how could it be as formidable as was Grendel?) – seek if you dare. Indeed, only Beowulf's (martial) counsel can now help – 'Nu is se ræd gelang / eft æt þe anum' (ll. 1376b–1377a). Hrothgar insists here that 'all depends' on Beowulf alone; moreover, he will of course reward Beowulf handsomely should Beowulf return from the mere.

While Hrothgar does not control Beowulf through well-established reciprocities, he does want to influence Beowulf here and recruit him for the task at hand – hence his pointed reference to the feud and to Beowulf's part in it, his emphasis on the great loss that Æschere's death is, and his forbidding characterization of the mere. Happily, this appeal is something to which Beowulf can immediately respond, proactively so to speak: 'don't sorrow wise warrior; it is better for each to avenge his friend than to mourn much. It is better that he who can works fame before he dies.' He promises to follow Grendel's kinswoman wherever she goes in the earth's embrace. Given that ringing vow, Hrothgar leaps up, in effect rejuvenated.

Although Beowulf's friendly arrival and query precipitated a mixed response, almost a rebuke in part, the departure from Heorot begins with high expectations, one supposes, now that Hrothgar has recruited Beowulf for this mission, eliciting from him a ringing, heroic maxim. Hrothgar rides out leading Geats and Danes, actively showing a rugged, narrow way to the mere's weird side. Their departure from the hall, begun in the energy of hope and thankfulness ('Ahleop ða se gomela, Gode þancode, / mihtigan Drihtne, þæs se man gespræc,' ll. 1396–7), slows down after we are told that the wise king, splendidly equipped, went forth; with him shield-bearers stepped forth also. This is Hrothgar as warrior-king, active, showing the way that Grendel's mother has apparently taken. Perhaps her underwater place is on that strange side of the mere.

Later, at the edge of the mere, Beowulf readies himself for an armed dive into the lake. His ringing words in the hall about seeking the mother monster wherever she might go could now find a more chastened form. After all, the grim shock upon arrival of finding Æschere's head at the cliff's edge above the mere has to have a sobering effect. The discovery is painful to the Danes ('Denum eallum wæs, / winum Scyldinga, weorce on mode,' ll. 1417b–1418b) and the mere itself is bubbling with gore. The Danes and Geats, those on foot, all sit down and stare at the strange water monsters and sea dragons in the mere, perhaps quite daunted by the ghastly theatre they have come upon. But then someone blows a war horn and the creatures thrash around in angry response, which incites a Geat bowman to shoot one, while others then grapple with it, using boar spears to land the terrible stranger ('gryrelicne gist,' l. 1441a). Perhaps this proof of ghastly mortality, fished out of the mere, is all Beowulf needs to begin preparing himself.

In the course of putting on helmet and armour, he accepts the battle-tested, war-famous, hereditary sword, Hrunting. We are told that Unferth does not call to mind those words he spoke earlier when, in the course of drinking, he challenged Beowulf. Now, we are told, he dares not risk his life, as he loans that blade to the better sword-warrior. For that he loses fame, doing so in effect for forgoing heroic deeds – that is, the attempt itself, however it turns, is worthy of fame. But Unferth does not lose fame and standing altogether. By accepting the sword and even calling upon it in his battle cry, Beowulf indirectly honours Unferth, the owner, who has martial status because of the sword in the first place; moreover, the sword is loaned, not given away or seized. Beowulf will have to return it if he can. But first he must say something now as he directly confronts the environment of monstrous creatures only verbally conjured up before. Has his boast altered in any way? Before departing into the mere, what are his thoughts and expectations?

He turns to Hrothgar: recall what we spoke of a while ago – that 'if I at *your need* [the emphasis is mine] should lose my life that you would to me ever be in a father's place. Be thou a protector to my hand-comrades if battle takes me' (ll. 1476–81). He implies an obligation in that if he fails he has failed not out of his own need but because of Hrothgar's need (using the same word that ethically pulled on him in his original decision to seek out Hroðgar because of the Grendel affair). Thus he can ask for the return favour of protection on behalf of his bereaved retainers. This is as much as Beowulf has so far acknowledged concerning Hroðgar's desire to be in a father's place to Beowulf – and only in this extremity. He would transfer that role, of adopted kinship, from himself to his retainers in the event of his death. He does go on to call Hroðgar beloved (*leofa*) but he does so only when arranging the sending of his treasures to Hygelac, who when he sees them will know that Beowulf found a good, munificent distributor of rings, a lord excellent in his customs ('gumcyst,' l. 1486a). Beowulf signifies the treasure only as his honourable deserts and as expressing Hroðgar's honour, his manly virtue, the best of his class (*cyst*). That emphasis conserves the field of honour between the two. And as for Unferth, that widely known man ('widcuðne man,' l. 1489b), Hroðgar should see that he gets the famous, serpentine-incised sword back, with which, Beowulf now declares, he will accomplish fame 'oþðe mec deað nimeð' (l. 1491b). By specifically mentioning Unferth and the sword here Beowulf finishes the closing of the breach between the two of them, a closing that has two movements – via Hrunting to Beowulf and then back again to Unferth. Hrunting is the peace-making medium here – as it were the loan of peace between the two, unequally inspired and unequally brave warriors.

On his long way to the bottom Beowulf's armour both helps him dive and protects him when Grendel's mother, the sea-wolf, seizes him, bringing her unwelcome guest into her dire, inhospitable underwater hall ('niðsele'). There Beowulf swings at her head with Hrunting, but he, the stranger (guest – 'gist'), discovers that the sword, that battle-light, bites not at all – the first time that battle-treasure failed. Beowulf quickly throws the weapon down and grabs the monster by her shoulder or perhaps her hair, as some have argued, pulling her down. She recovers and turns in such a way as to throw Beowulf to the ground, he now being somewhat weary. She somehow suppresses her 'hall-guest' ('selegyst') and tries stabbing him with her seax (a short sword). His armour deflects her thrust, especially his corselet does, and then somehow he stands up and sees a gigantic, giant-made sword, which he seizes and with which he strikes, cutting her lethally through the neck. The host-guest relationship here has been an especially parodic, violent, and perhaps even an obscene and insulting one on both sides.[12] With the sword in hand he then searches the horrible hall for Grendel, whom he finds dead and whom he beheads to be sure as well as to provide him with an unmistakable trophy. That beheading melts the sword's blade in Grendel's still corrosive blood, sending gore out of the hall and up into the mere, where it comes to the surface and is interpreted as meaning that Beowulf has been destroyed. The Danes eventually leave the Geats sitting, strangers (guests – 'Gistas setan / modes seoce,' ll. 1602b–1603a) sick in mind, staring at the mere, perhaps waiting for Beowulf's body or some part of him to emerge, perhaps simply unable to do more than mourn for their apparently slain lord, wishing without hope that they might see him again. When Beowulf in fact emerges from the mere, having returned triumphantly, he who now has purged the waters and brought two trophies to the surface – Grendel's head and the great sword hilt – his Geats gather around joyfully and thank God. They then all set out, carrying the huge head with some difficulty, back to Heorot. He has left one environment, entered a hostile one, departed from that with trophies of victory and now arrives among his joyful warrior crew. From Beowulf's morning arrival at Heorot to his emergence from the mere, the poet has given us a spectacular, emotionally wrenching set of arrivals and departures, and arrival again.

When Beowulf returns to Heorot, bringing Grendel's head and the ancient sword hilt (the blade having melted in Grendel's still hot blood), he says that he and the Geats have with pleasure (*lust*, l. 1653b) 'brought' that 'sea-booty' to Hrothgar – Healfdene's son and man of the Scyldings. By bringing something to Hrothgar he hardly returns as Hrothgar's equal, rather as a warrior and monster-slaying supplicant, bringing his grisly treasure from the bottom of the mere. He adds definitively that the Danes need no longer fear death from that side (the Grendel side) again. This pleasure Beowulf speaks of, however, is nothing more than open and friendly. It carries no further obligations or intentions, although it no doubt looks for a return.

The unlooked for, amazing arrival of Beowulf and the Geats requires something major from Hrothgar, who along with the rest of the Danes had assumed the worst when seeing blood well up from the mere. Now, in his most meditative mood, Hrothgar accepts the sword hilt, reads the runes inscribed thereon, which tell of the flood, for whom the sword was made and how the eternal Lord slew a race of giants. That divine requital by deluge perhaps leads him to think of Beowulf and the vanquishing under water of the Grendel kin. He then pronounces Beowulf's widely spread 'glory,' 'vigour' and 'renown' (all signified by 'blæd,' l. 1703b), along with his strength and wisdom. Moreover, Hrothgar promises to uphold his friendship and offer of reward, as he indicated earlier when urging Beowulf to the feud-work of seeking Grendel's mother. This is of course what he must do as an ethical king. What he still wants, however, is what he indicated earlier in his adoption speech and in the giving of the great treasures. But what he seems to have accepted is that Beowulf will not join the Danes by taking up a leading place in their line of succession. For he now announces that Beowulf in his might and wisdom will be 'a long lasting comfort to his own people, a help to warriors: 'Đu scealt to frofre weorþan / eal langtwidig leodum þinum, / hæleðum to helpe' (ll. 1707b–1709a). Beowulf will be a lasting, protective, and consoling 'help' to his people and warriors – reflecting both *gravitas* insofar as he is a solace ('frofor') for his people and *celeritas* in that he martially protects and helps warriors.

That acceptance in part may inform Hrothgar's further meditation and advice – his so-called sermon. Much *Beowulf* criticism sees that homiletically tinged speech in thematic terms and as ethically or else even spiritually central to the poem – as some version of the theme of reversal or the theme of the opposition of good and evil or both.[13] The issue of pride emerges and is sometimes interpreted at Beowulf's expense. But dramatically and politically, Hrothgar's speech has a largely overlooked emotional and social context: his quite recent, even fervent hope that Beowulf will somehow join him in extended sovereignty and help secure a fruitful, Danish future. The immediate turn from praise of Beowulf involves a recollection of Heremod, who was not such a help to the Honor-Scyldings, the sons of Ecgwala. The Heremod story moves Hrothgar into a general meditation on how many gifts God can give a man and yet that man can forget God and his fortunate self, become unmindful of present and future, and have awakened in him a proud, greedy demon. He turns from this directly to Beowulf, this great warrior who apparently has side-stepped his offer of close kinship and recruitment, to offer advice. Calling Beowulf 'dear,' he recommends that Beowulf protect himself, choose the better, that is, eternal fame and eschew excessive pride. He would in his aged wisdom instruct Beowulf in the vicissitudes of life. Although Beowulf is now prosperous in his strength, there are many ways of dying in the world – by sword, fire, flood, spear, or just hateful old age. This final gift of cautionary wisdom is something Hrothgar can give even if Beowulf has not accepted Hrothgar's deepest offer. Hrothgar then turns to himself, to his own reversals in a long life: first great success in war and the protection of his people, such that he thought he had no enemy under the sky, then Grendel and great sorrow, grief after mirth and song. His kingly rule has been a martially vigorous one, much celebrated in the hall, until Grendel. His *celeritas* – productive of victories and song – is so suddenly drawn up short that the reversal is in effect inexplicable; but then reversal comes again as the very personal invasion (he says Grendel is his own 'ingenga') is overturned with Grendel's defeat such that he can see with his own eyes that bloody head, for which victory he thanks God and invites Beowulf to a victory banquet. Hrothgar presents prosperity and suffering, the great reversals in his life, as first-person events, as his own. This too is the power of the Danish king – to prosper greatly and to suffer greatly. He also emphasizes the personal here because he has let go of his desire to recruit Beowulf and thereby repair the Danish kingship he occupies.

Nevertheless, his is still the power to command as he tells Beowulf to go now to the banquet and the treasure sharing. His is a *gravitas* extensively shaped by long years, by sorrowful experience and by wisdom; yet still he is a power, he has a touch of *celeritas*, in that he has survived bitter reversals. At this point the pathos of his address is that he thinks Beowulf will simply exult in his gifts and return to his lord and uncle, to his people. Indeed, that is how the poet seems to express the matter when he tells us that Beowulf was 'shiningly gracious at heart when he went quickly to seek his bench as Hrothgar, the wise one, had commanded' ('Geat wæs glædmod, geong sona to, / setles neosan, swa se snottra heht,' ll. 1785–6). While still with the power to command and dispose, Hrothgar is alone and has no reason to think that this beloved Beowulf will serve or join him in any further way. His great gifts have been openly accepted and a kind of temporary obligation sprung from the mother's revenge has been fulfilled. Imagine his surprise when in the morning Beowulf, taking his leave as might be expected, makes a spectacular offer.

Beowulf and his Geats are eager to seek out their ship and return home. But first there is unfinished business: whatever Hrothgar may think now, his offer of the succession and thus a dynamic share in Danish sovereignty still hangs in the air; moreover, Beowulf still has Unferth's sword, Hrunting. He bids Unferth take the sword, thanking him for the loan. He praises that dear iron, accounting it good in battle (after all, it did not break). Beowulf then goes to the high seat and greets Hrothgar, saying that now they would seek out Hygelac. They have been here well attended to in all desirable and good things; 'you, Hrothgar, have treated us well, open-handedly.' Beowulf could stop here with his formally cadenced, possibly intense rhetoric of honorable treatment – 'Wæron her tela, / willum bewenede; þu us wel dohtest' (ll. 1820b–1821).[14] Beowulf could now simply, politely await Hrothgar's good wishes before leaving the hall. However, he offers a remarkable gift: military aid if he learns that he might strive for even more of Hrothgar's 'mind-love' than he has already received because of his war deeds. Beowulf's use of 'modlufan' (l. 1823a) is a breakthrough of sorts for Hrothgar, seeming to indicate Beowulf's warm appreciation of Hrothgar's emotive attentions. Should he learn of Hrothgar's needs (again, an ethical call) he will quickly ready himself. Indeed, if he learns that enemies threaten Hrothgar, as has been the case in the past, Beowulf will bring thousands of warriors to Hrothgar's aid. And although his own lord, Hygelac, is young, Beowulf knows that the lord of the Geats will support him in words and works such that Beowulf can further honour Hrothgar and bring aid – the spear shaft in strong support, 'there where Hrothgar has need of men,' (as he just did a few days before against Grendel). Invoking Hygelac as a second to his promise asserts that he is not just saying things. Moreover, Hrethric (but apparently not Hrothgar's other son, Hrothmund, for some reason) will be welcome should he come to visit.

In itself this is an extraordinary, new commitment, given that Beowulf first comes to the Danes uninvited and now, in just three days, has performed tremendous feats on behalf of the Danes, for which he has been magnificently and leadingly rewarded. Beowulf here, by the unlooked for gift of this offer, in part acknowledges the dimensions of Hrothgar's gift-giving. Unlike Mary Dockray-Miller, and to a much lesser extent Tom Shippey,[15] I don't see Beowulf here as asserting his power and status, as being somewhat arrogant or as implying that the Geatish hall can protect Hrethric better than Hrothgar can in Heorot. Beowulf knows that such a promise is an alliance, establishing a *mutuality* of asymmetrical or else supportive relations (clear in his prepositional use of 'helpe,' l. 1830a, varied by 'protection,' 'geoce,' l. 1834 – this would be help and protection offered up to Hrothgar), and 'herige,' 'honour.' Moreover, these notes are amplified in Hrothgar's expansion and characterization of this new relationship. Still, by implying that Hrothgar may need help, his point could become 'intrinsically face-threatening,' something he softens, according to Shippey,[16] by making his offer look self-interested, saying Hrothgar has needed help before, as though in the natural course of world affairs, and by suggesting that the offer comes in some way from Hygelac, not himself (he can only *know* that Hygelac will support such aid if Hygelac has so indicated somehow). On balance, however, I think his insistence on the pronouns 'you' and 'I' marks this alliance as mainly between Hrothgar and himself. He does not pointedly include the Danes generally because he cannot establish an alliance between two peoples; his is a martial commitment between two men, which he claims Hygelac will support in a bond of word and deed. While not accepting 'adoption' or spiritual kinship, Beowulf does here establish a 'kinship' of aid, of both direct and collateral support. That kinship does, however, embrace Hrothgar's son in a general amity. If Hrethric, a princely son, should seek the hall of the Geats, Beowulf adds that he will there find many friends and protectors – for it is better to seek distant lands for him who trusts in himself (apparently the less than manly stay home).[17]

In answer, Hrothgar waxes nearly ecstatic before bringing his power to bear and greatly enlarging Beowulf's offer: 'the wise Lord has sent that speech into your mind!' Hrothgar cannot have expected anything of this sort from the formally departing Beowulf. Indeed, he has never heard 'wiser thought or settlement' ('þingian,' l. 1843b) before in one so young of age. He pronounces Beowulf's definitive features in consequence: 'Þu eart mægenes strang, ond on mode frod, wis wordcwide!' ('you are strong in might and in mind mature, wise in speech'). Hrothgar, as Beowulf did, emphasizes the person-to-person, face-to-face nature of this commitment: I to you; you to me (this personal tie does of course permit relations of mutuality bètween the two peoples – a door Beowulf clearly opens when he invites Hrethric). Hrothgar, again, does not expect now to recruit Beowulf or to adopt this great warrior. Indeed, he expects that should the spear take Hygelac, Hrethel's offspring, or sickness or sword do the same – and here Hrothgar repeats part of his litany of the ways of dying; should your prince die and you still live, 'the Sea-Geats would not have a better warrior to choose as king, as hoard-guardian of warriors if you would hold the kinsmen's kingdom' (ll. 1850–1853a).

Because he reprises part of his own speech on unlooked for deaths, Hrothgar anticipates such a possibility purely as part of a world of sudden reversal (even Beowulf might die before receiving an offer of the Geatish throne), not as something that would necessarily happen politically. He also both honours Beowulf absolutely here, judiciously; and he acknowledges Beowulf's own strength of mind – such that he might not accept an offer of the kingship. Again, his speech is pronoun pointed – if your lord dies and you have your life and if you are willing. By direct address he continues to emphasize the personal here, turning again to his own estimation of this beloved Beowulf ('leofa Beowulf,' l. 1854b), whose mind and spirit please him ever more. For, he proclaims, Beowulf has personally, through his magnificent offer, opened the way to a mutuality of kinship and peace ('sib gemæne,' l. 1857a) between the people of the Geats and the Spear-Danes; Beowulf has set strife to rest, the enmity ('inwitniþas,' l. 1858a) that once occupied Danes and Geats (presumably in some past well before Beowulf's arrival, although that enmity may not have been *between* the two peoples, as Chickering argues).[18] Hrothgar inhabits this wonderful development, putting the great weight of his rule behind an expansion – not just rest and lack of strife or contentiousness ('sacu,' l. 1857b); rather he announces deep amity through continuing gift exchange ('maþmas gemæne,' 'lac ond luftacen,' ll. 1860a, 1863a). He expands Beowulf's military and political offer into a complete mutuality of exchange and love between the two peoples for as long as he rules the wide kingdom. This is what Hrothgar can do and Beowulf cannot. He finishes by formally, even legalistically, saying that he knows the people will firmly keep to good traditions 'with friends and against foes.'[19] Hrothgar is blameless in every way, wise as of old. He brings his full power as a great king, an establisher of reciprocity and a legislator to this new amity as he much enlarges Beowulf's surprise offer.

This exchange between Beowulf and Hrothgar essentially crafts a new arrangement – one of complete mutuality between the two of them and between their peoples. To honour Beowulf for this development, Hrothgar gives him twelve more treasures and bids that he with those goods seek his people in health and safety and return again quickly – 'snude eft cuman' (l. 1869b). At this point, with the thought of Beowulf's departure and hope for his speedy return, Hrothgar becomes emotional at a personal level. The most intelligent, professional as well as provocative analysis of this passage is Mary

Dockray-Miller's speculative discussion of Hrothgar's loss of masculinity – that his actions fall 'outside the bounds of "heroic life," that to cry, embrace, and kiss at a farewell are distinctly non-heroic gestures that indicate desperation rather than resolution. Nowhere else in Old English poetry do men display such overt emotion towards each other.'[20] Dockray-Miller is right about the unique nature of this moment in the literature (although life may have been different). But even in this poem strong characters will have intensely human moments: Hygelac, certainly an aggressive warrior king, will be intensely curious when Beowulf arrives from Heorot (l. 1985a); Beowulf himself will have strong, uncustomary emotions and thoughts in the aftermath of the dragon's attack (l. 2328); and Wiglaf will sit, weary and fatigued, by Beowulf's shoulder, trying to rouse him with water (ll. 2852–4), while Geat nobility will go heavy-eyed with the messenger to the place where their king and dragon lie dead. Moreover, in *The Battle of Maldon* the aged Byrhtwold, along with those famous lines about heart being the keener and courage greater as strength lessens, movingly proposes to lie down beside his 'dearly beloved,' dead lord (ll. 318–19). We have so little heroic poetry outside of *Beowulf* that what is in *Beowulf* may well reflect the normative possibilities of emotion in heroic life literarily rendered, whereas story and verse outside of the poem in the main reflect the political projects of lordship and kingship in late Anglo-Saxon England.[21] Still, the combination of gesture and intense emotion is unusual in this passage. How is it presented to us and what can we say about its inspiriting causes?

The developing, ongoing background takes us from Hrothgar's first celebration of victory in Heorot, when he refers to Beowulf as, essentially, a god-blest warrior who has with God's aid done what the Danes could not do; then he offers a new, heart-felt kinship with Beowulf and urges that Beowulf hold it well; next he and Beowulf have come to call each other 'beloved' or 'dear' and Beowulf asks that Hrothgar stand in a father's place to his retainers should he, Beowulf, die in battle with Grendel's mother. After bringing Grendel's head and the gigantic sword hilt back to Heorot, Beowulf receives Hrothgar's great praise and his disappointed acceptance of Beowulf's unbending tie to Hygelac and the Geats. When Beowulf the next morning invokes Hrothgar's 'mind love' and offers a military alliance, Hrothgar with great pleasure reveals his growing admiration for the beloved Beowulf's extraordinary qualities. In these developments we have the mainspring of Hrothgar's access to high emotion in the leave-taking scene. Those feelings do not come upon him suddenly, from out of nowhere.

The poet also sets up the scene by having Hrothgar command and dispose material goods in the hall – especially those twelve treasures added to Beowulf's already magnificent compensation. He then calls Hrothgar a king good in his nobility ('cyning æþelum god, l. 1870b), lord of the Scyldings, as he narrates Hrothgar's embrace and kiss of the 'best' of thanes. As Mary Dockray-Miller notes in a nice touch, kisses in Old English texts need have nothing erotic or pathetic in them: 'Saints kiss their followers, kisses of peace seal treaties.'[22] Indeed, a kiss is more than likely to have hierarchical implications. The good *king* kisses the best of thanes; then tears rush from him, the grey-haired one (tears usually signify grief in Old English texts, although in *Elene* there are tears of triumph). Here Dockray-Miller discusses a potentially telling connection, given the compound 'blondenfeax' (l. 1873). The term applies to Hrothgar elsewhere and also to Ongentheow, arguably a hyper-masculine king who vigorously defends his homeland and terrifyingly threatens surrounded Geats at Ravenswood. He is always a terror king of sorts, not like the aged Hrothgar we see in the aftermath of Grendel's raids. Indeed, Ongentheow is more like Hrothgar's predecessors, who terrorized their neighbours into submission (especially so with Scyld Scefing). One can accept this contrast as part of Dockray-Miller's argument and still see Hrothgar as other than lesser or even empty in his masculinity. He is grey-haired, for example, in the passage earlier when he probably thinks along with other elders that Beowulf will not return from the mere, given the blood welling up from its depths. After the ninth hour, the Danes leave, led by the gold-giver of men. The Geats stay behind, sick in mind, which is how the gold-giver of men probably feels as well. His 'masculinity' here is of course not the narrow vein of asserting his authority or physical power over others but rather of the power of decision. Elsewhere, he is marked as grey-haired when he seeks his bed the night after Beowulf's return from the mere. Dockray-Miller aptly notes these passages in the course of indicating that Hrothgar does not participate in the 'masculine' behaviour of the warriors who stay in the hall, arms at the ready. This point taken, we still have a conception of Hrothgar that gives him the distant credit always of having once been a vigorous battle king (ll. 64–67a), of being lord of the (valiant) Scyldings and then a different sort of king: a legislator par excellence, good in his nobility.

What Hrothgar is said to feel strongly in this scene is something he has felt before: loss in the thought that Beowulf will not return soon enough; that he will not see Beowulf again – as at the edge of the mere a few hundred lines earlier. I accept Dockray-Miller's very nice rendering of the lines of longing: convincingly she would have Hrothgar's 'spirit (with heart-bonds fast because of the dear man)' secretly long for Beowulf – a longing in his blood. Does this make him weak? Does he long 'not just for Beowulf's approval and acceptance but for the power implicit in becoming the father of the powerful son?'[23] Certainly those tears and that longing do not make Beowulf and Hrothgar like emotional brothers in arms.[24] Rather, Hrothgar feels this moment keenly: he has come to love Beowulf dearly; a day or two ago he thought Beowulf would not return from the bloody mere; and he has been more than happily surprised by Beowulf's offer of military alliance.

In letting Beowulf go, now he cannot restrain his tears, although he does not voice his burning love for Beowulf. His are tears, I would say, simply of love, longing, and the grievous thought that he will not see Beowulf again (much as Geats weep after the messenger's hateful speech late in the poem ['wollenteare,' l. 3032a]); tears do not diminish Hrothgar's nobility or his wisdom. Indeed, when Beowulf leaves without tears and exulting in his treasures – the active pleasure of a hugely successful young man yet to lose anyone close to him – we learn that the Geats praised Hrothgar's gifts. The poet adds that Hrothgar was a 'peerless' king ('an cyning') in nothing blameless, although age deprives him of joyful strength, much as it injures or harms many (ll. 1885b–1887). One can easily imagine the poet saying something similar of an aged King Alfred, someone for whom kingship, if we can trust his additions to the translation of Boethius's *Consolation*, was less about ambition or material gain than about wisdom, virtue, and the fitting administration of authority, where, as Charles Plummer would have it, 'a king's raw material and instruments of rule are a well-peopled land, and he must have men of prayer, men of war, and men of work.'[25]

Masculinity in the active, battle-seeking sense of course is something Hrothgar's age eliminates (as happens for many, although not for Beowulf or Ongentheow). The major field of masculine activity left to him is the hall, the showing of regal presence, the receiving of others and their trophies, gestures of giving and command, the power to enlarge offers or not. Here Hrothgar is both venerable and, if we use Klaeber's translation of 'an,' peerless. Emotionally, Hrothgar's masculinity evolves in his deepening feelings for Beowulf – a 'son' he would dearly love to adopt, to foster as someone upon whom to devolve his residual war functions (hence the war-saddle as one of his gifts). In his proffered but unaccepted effort at heroic fatherhood, Hrothgar of course fails to secure an immediate devolution of his martial function – on this point I can sympathize with some of the tenor of critiques that see Hrothgar as passive, as impotent in some sense in contrast to Beowulf. And he would certainly lose masculine standing, as Mary Dockray-Miller argues – if, that is, masculinity is entirely a matter of naked, martial prowess and we see Hrothgar in the farewell scene as attempting a 'last-ditch' assertion of said masculinity 'by playing the role of Father to Beowulf as son.' From an invoked Lacanian perspective, Dockray-Miller would argue that 'if Hrothgar is *not* the Father, he does not have the phallus. He does not determine signification and metaphor. He does not control the Law, the imposition of cultural norms. He can see himself in the position of powerful masculinity, in the position of Fatherhood, but is not actually there.'[26]

While I am uncertain how to proceed in Lacanian terms, I would say that Hrothgar makes no 'last ditch' effort here, that he has already accepted Beowulf's intense loyalty to his own lord and uncle, Hygelac. Moreover, the poem clearly establishes Hrothgar initially as possessor of 'the phallus' insofar as he thrives in war and peace, commands the building of Heorot, names the hall, and therein practices well the customary munificence that falls to him as 'sitting' king, in *gravitas*. So to speak, having established the law of the phallus, he in fact upholds cultural norms he instantiates in his naming activity (giving his great hall a name) and in his declared sharing of everything except the lives of his people and the commons. He does not lose that position simply because he no longer rides out as a war-king or because he and the Danes avoid Grendel's carnage by sleeping elsewhere, rather than in the hall. After bloody failures, such an arrangement is certainly prudent, something a peoples' protector ought to recommend, leading by regal example. Moreover, in Heorot by day, by upholding all good customs, by distributing goods and by enlarging offers and having goods and aid come to him – as would be the case in fully mutual exchange with the Geats – he continually re-enacts what we can call a sitting masculinity, say, if we like, the administration of 'the phallus.' But the more local point I think is that the deepening of feelings for Beowulf is as much a part of heroic life in the poem as is gift giving and warrior leadership. There is no 'effeminate irrelevance'[27] in Hrothgar's emotions, any more than in Hygelac's and Beowulf's later – only the emotional deepening of *gravitas*.

CHAPTER FOUR

Beowulf's Homecoming with 'Celeritas' and Loyalty

Beowulf's homecoming receives a mainly perfunctory response from readers, at least for the passages not concerned with the Hygd-Modthryth comparison or Beowulf's anticipation of feud in his account of the prospective marriage, arranged by Hrothgar, between Freawaru and Ingeld. Readers have also responded to Beowulf's retelling of events, their interest focusing almost exclusively on his skills as an oral teller or narrator or as an entertainer in the hall.[1] But even the sections involving travel, reception, and greeting require careful attention. They are not transitional and are socially more dynamic than they seem when read as type scenes, for example 'hero on the beach' (again), or as conventional greeting and response. A further problem arises in *Beowulf* translation, for any passage, when we insist on fluent, modern word order and look for approximate sense as a way to conserve something of the original's alliterative prosody. We are prone to lose touch with the social or else formal and ritualistic force of the moment – a problem that plagues the vast major-ity of poetical translations and even troubles prose renderings, where there is more syntactic flexibility usually and thus more likelihood of rendering the half-line by half-line movement, suspensions, and emphases of the original.

So how is an amazingly successful hero received by his great kinsman, his mother's brother and personal lord? And how does such a hero move and present himself? First of course the return of this beloved man and his men has been eagerly looked for by the coast watch, no doubt set there by Hygelac. Beowulf has the ship in which he and his men return pulled up to the beach, secured and then unloaded of its treasures. Does he now saunter directly into Hygelac's hall and announce his successes? Does he come full of pride and even somewhat cockily? And what might be on Hygelac's mind once he hears of his powerful retainer's return, who of course is special to him for also being his sister's son?

Certainly Beowulf does not saunter in – there is nothing of the late, adolescent jock about him. In fact, while eventually he and his men are said to move quickly over the sand to Hygelac's fort and hall, their movement is narratively delayed by the so-called Modthryth digression, a passage apparently motivated in part by a desire to contrast Hygelac's young queen, Hygd, – that young, wise queen, Hæreth's daughter – with the once notorious Modthryth (who had suitors slain until her father successfully married her to the continental king, Offa, with whom she lived in high love and had a son). Many readers have taken this passage as an unfortunate interpolation, somewhat crude, perhaps even an excrescence.[2] Certainly it may be an interpolation, in honour perhaps of the Mercian Offa (early to mid-eighth century) in whose court some version of *Beowulf* might well have been recited before acquiring its late West Saxon dialect. But if interpolated, why just here? Mention of Hygd at any point might inspire the passage.

If we think of Beowulf's homecoming as requiring a marriage of the formal and the eager, delaying his approach to Hygelac's fortified enclosure is good strategy, elevating the sense of approach and indicating that Beowulf returns to a regal hall, to a powerful lord and a young queen with their own, stressed associations and therein extended being. The land of the Geats is no flat, grey place gone still in Beowulf's absence. It is the home of a young, wise queen with her own lineage and of a great lord called Ongentheow's slayer. When in fitt 28 the poet's verbs pick Beowulf up again, it is as though he has been suspended temporarily in the act of commanding the bringing up from the ship of treasures and plated gold. Beowulf 'departed then, the hardy, tempered one with his hand companions, his own, over the sand, the seashore; he traversed, walked upon, the wide shore.' We need redundancy in our translations and the awkwardness of extended phrasings to suggest that this movement is neither perfunctory nor a kind of race, although it is performed energetically, with some speed. Moreover, we are told that 'the world candle shone, bright from the south.' Given the repeated association of light and sun with victory elsewhere in *Beowulf*, we can take this reference as something more than a weather report. The poet underlines Beowulf's victory-enhanced movement here. His is a victory trot, perhaps in lively, quick time, but not a parade. In a phrase – 'Hi sið drugon,' l. 1966b – the poet tells us that Beowulf and his men performed their travel, went valorously across the beach to where Hygelac presides in his gift giving. They have, then, an accomplished and martial air about them in this their victorious return.

This eagerly awaited and then busily received arrival is high energy, more so than any other warrior arrival in the poem. Hygelac was of Beowulf's arrival quickly informed, that 'there into the homestead, the protector of warriors, shield companion, living has come, sound from battle, unto the hall. Quickly was made ready, as the lord commanded, for the foot-guests, the hall's interior.' 'Hraðe wæs gerymed, swa se rica bebead, / feðegestum flet innanweard' (ll. 1975–6). Here the inversions and suspensions function to emphasize side by side and through half-line positions first the glorious arrival, living, of that great shield companion and then the force of Hygelac's command: quickly was made ready, for the foot-guests, the hall's interior. These returning Geats are in some provisional way 'foot-guests,' or perhaps better, 'pacing guests,' to be honoured, made welcome as a guest would be rather than welcomed as merely familiar retainers. As guests they are potentially strangers and they need to be questioned.

They have returned in high, martial spirits – but have they returned quite as they left? Have they changed in any way? Hygelac does not bustle; nor does he simply rise from his place in the hall and greet. He is excited and commands a great honouring of the arriving troop. 'Sat then by themselves he who battle survived, kinsman with kinsman, after the lord of men through ceremonious speech formally greeted [his lord], with earnest, reciprocally loyal ['hold'], forceful words; with meadcups in hand, to pour, circling around that hall was Hæreth's daughter, loved by the people.' 'Gesæt þa wið sylfne se ða sæcce genaes, / mæg wið mæge, syððan mandryhten / þurh hleoðorcwyde holdne gegrette, / meaglum wordum' (ll. 1977–1980a).

Those snippets, as though panned by a camera, both indicate the ritual formality of the moment and provide a transition between Beowulf's ceremonious, loyalty-expressing, hearty greeting and Hygelac's complex reply. That the two kinsmen sit side by side is notable as well. The last time two kinsmen sat next to or near each other was in Heorot – Hrothgar and Hrothulf, also uncle and nephew, although Hrothulf is a brother's, not a sister's, son. Hrothgar and Hrothulf are friendly, the context suggests, although most readers assume tension underlying their relationship, such that after Hrothgar's death Hrothulf will usurp the throne rather than serve as protector for one of Hrothgar's sons. Whether that is the poet's implication or not, the present moment between Beowulf and Hygelac is not yet entirely transparent.

At the stressed beginning of the b half line, the poet places Hygelac, who begins to question his companion in the high hall, and is intensely eager to know ('fyrwit bræc') about the sea-Geats journey: 'what befell you on that journey, dear Beowulf?' Although he uses the endearment – 'leofa Beowulf' – Hygelac's desire to know here is not mere curiosity, which is how nearly all translations render it; nor is it Heaney's lame 'hankering to know.' Hygelac's desire is more like Constance Hieatt's 'burned with curiosity' or Francis Gummere's 'sore longing,' or even Garmonsway and Simpson's old-fashioned 'pricked him.'[3] What thoughts would be intensely forming here in Hygelac's mind? What does he badly want or need to know? Surely Hygelac has heard the news of Beowulf's great victories – news Beowulf will characterize as no secret ('undyrne,' much as news of Grendel's depredations reached the Geats and much as news of Beowulf's death will reach the Franks and Frisians). Many men know of the great meeting ('[micel] gemeting,' l. 2001), that time of battle between ourselves, he adds, in that place where Grendel accomplished much sorrow for the Victory-Scyldings, misery for a long time. Of course no matter how fast or far such news travels, it is not real and present until Beowulf himself narrates some version of it. Still, Hygelac needs to hear more than entertaining tales from across the sea.

First he asks if Beowulf settled ('gebettest,' as in settling a feud or punishing a crime) Hrothgar's widely known sorrow, adding that he did not trust that voyage in the first place, when Beowulf suddenly (implying potentially disastrously) resolved upon it. 'Ic ðæs modceare / sorhwylmum seað, siðe ne truwode / leofes mannes' (ll. 1992b–1994a). Whelming sorrow or worry seathed within him, he now asserts, although he thinks of Beowulf as having left to perform a lawful deed. Nevertheless, his feelings were not mild or, one imagines, unexpressed. In fact he says that he long urged Beowulf not to go and greet that slaughter Spirit (apparently in this relationship his is not to command). But because the enormously powerful Beowulf would go, having been moved ethically to do so because Hrothgar needed the help of men in the Grendel affair, and because he may have gone with his deep luck as read in the casting of omens, Hygelac's whelming sorrow and distrust then are put aside. No wonder that now, in prominent, stressed position, he wisely thanks God: 'Gode ic þanc secge, / þæs ðe ic ðe gesundne geseon moste' (ll. 1997b–1998).'God I thanks now say that I you sound see may.' If we smooth this out we miss the expostulatory force involving God and Hygelac's intense gratefulness, as well as its central object, Beowulf, whom Hygelac can now see again. But still, glad as he is, grateful as he is, what does he need to know about Beowulf's adventures and about Beowulf himself?

The latter issue – what about Beowulf – that is what intensely churns in his mind, and one could say torments him. There may well be a touch of foreboding in that curiosity also, if we consider an Old Norse cognate for 'fyrwit' ('fyrir-vissa'). For why else mention earlier sorrow and worry at all if it is not some kind of rebuke or wonder or worry in the present? He knows what Beowulf has done – report has preceded him and his victorious arrival home says much. But he says he did not trust that venture; he long urged that Beowulf not approach that slaughter-spirit, leave him to the South-Danes, which in retrospect deepens the context within which Beowulf decided to act; he responded to an ethical call, Hrothgar's need, and to the casting of omens by Geatish wisemen for whom Beowulf was dear – they did not dissuade him and that showing of deep luck must have set Hygelac aback, while clearly not lessening his worries.

Having now voiced them again, his present, intense desire must differ from his feelings shortly before Beowulf left three or so days ago. Now he needs to know just how, with what loyalties and commitments, urges, and intentions has Beowulf left the Danes and returned to the Geats? Has this dearly beloved Beowulf returned, at the least, less impetuous? Less sudden in his resolutions? Or perhaps, and this is something one cannot even bear to think out loud, has Beowulf returned now somehow compromised in his loyalties, having performed *repeated* services for Hrothgar and the Danes? A singular service can be passed over as a kind of situational favour, for which a reward is appropriate; a second service suggests obligation incurred by that reward as well as further rewards. Ongoing reciprocity has materialized then, the breaking off of which could be construed as hostile, the continuing of which could be construed as shifting one's loyalties.

Beowulf's long reply is a complex performance, which includes his view of Danish-Heathobard relations in the Freawaru-Ingeld alliance, a baroque account of Grendel and his huge glove, an account of old and sad song in Heorot, and then an account of the monster mother's appearance, which generates that crucial question – has repeated service compromised Beowulf's loyalty? Thus just here he claims a lamentably aged Hrothgar's deeply sorrowful appeal, by Hygelac's life, ('Þa se ðeoden mec ðine life / healsode hreohmod,' ll. 2131–2132a) that he, Beowulf, take revenge on her. Beowulf ends with a final assertion that Hrothgar rewarded him with treasures unto his own keeping – 'ac he me (maðma)s geaf, / sunu Healfdenes on (min)ne sylfes dom' (ll. 2146b–2147).

The asserted appeal touches the issue of repeated service, and the claim about self-judgment crucially defines Hrothgar's rewards as having come into Beowulf's keeping of their own accord, rather than having been given with obligations attached: compare uses of the phrase in the Sigemund story and when Wiglaf gathers up treasure from the dragon's barrow (ll. 895, 2776).[4] Of course, Hrothgar never did appeal to Beowulf by way of Hygelac. And while many of the details Beowulf mentions in his rough and somewhat conflated overview of the fights might be unexceptionable (with conflation itself being a strategy) – such as Grendel's dragon-skin pouch and the kinds of songs and tales told in Heorot – the attribution of a specific locution is something else again, something he invents for his own purposes given the social nexus he has come home to: a very near past where a notable, public recruitment offer took place and an immediate present where his obligation to his uncle and lord needs restating such that any flicker of worry or doubt is extinguished, utterly. Inventing Hrothgar's plea is one of several moves by which Beowulf would dissipate any implication that his repeated services for the Danes have in any way compromised his loyal devotion to Hygelac and the Geats.

In Heorot, Beowulf says, he greeted Hrothgar upon arriving, who, once he knew Beowulf's mental spirit and intention, gave Beowulf a seat next to his sons (something Hrothgar does not do until after the Grendel fight, as part of his attempt to adopt Beowulf in spirit and recruit him materially). This early placement on Beowulf's part de-emphasizes both the stages of his several arrivals in the hall and the significance of that seating later, thus minimizing that gesture on Hrothgar's part after the Grendel fight.

When Beowulf talks about Wealhtheow, that famous queen, moving diplomatically several times in her circuit around the hall, he describes her as urging the peace-kinship pledge ('friðusibb folca,' l. 2017a) on behalf of her young sons and giving bracelets to warriors. He does not mention her sacred move with the *ful* directly toward himself. Instead he introduces Freawaru, Hrothgar's daughter, as another dispenser of harmony in the hall, while he anticipates at length what he thinks will happen when Hrothgar, after accepting advice about how to settle a slaughter feud with the Heathobards, attempts a marriage alliance with Ingeld through Freawaru. Here Beowulf produces a gnomic truth: 'Seldom there where the people have experienced calamity will the death spear bow for long, however good the bride.' Hrothgar's studied, overt, even potentially promising vision in this matter will come to naught, Beowulf thinks.

Indicating as much is Beowulf's indirect way of saying that whatever in his own, perhaps parallel case (one of recruitment, not alliance), whatever Hrothgar hoped for has also come to naught (although, as we saw, Beowulf has promised Hrothgar a military alliance and Hrothgar has announced continuing exchange). After Beowulf fills out what he supposes will happen at the wedding feast, he tells Hygelac about the Grendel fight, the swallowing of Hondscio, and that Grendel thought to do more, summarized thus: he, the bloody-toothed one, thought to try my strength. His ready claw grabbed me and he presumed to stuff me, sinless, into his large, cunningly wrought, dragon-skin pouch, [a Pagan-Dior, so to speak]! I thought that cannot be and so 'in anger upright I stood.'

He could have gone directly from mention of Freawaru, and his gnomic expectation that the marriage will fail bloodily, to nightfall and his preparations for Grendel. However, he delays getting to the dramatic struggle between himself and the monster to lay out a scenario for just how he supposes matters will turn when the Danish wedding party arrives and is well received by the Heathobards. Wearing the weapons of slain Heathobards, the Danish party will inevitably provoke comment and aggrieved thoughts – especially on the part of an old warrior who will point out to a young warrior the ancestral weapon a Dane sports, which weapon rightly should be the warrior's, having been his father's. Eventually the old spear warrior works his way into the mind of the young warrior, who will take revenge at night, his bloody act effectively dissolving the wedding festivities and causing Ingeld's love for his young bride to cool. Beowulf even seems to sympathize to some extent with the Heathobard side, as I argue elsewhere.[5] His rendition of what is likely to occur is usually taken as evidence of his maturing sense of the world, which it might be, but which he does not need to parade right now. What, then, might he be doing here for Hygelac's benefit? Why slow down the story Hygelac has asked about? Instead of recounting the diplomacy of the hall and the regal way in which Hrothgar turned Heorot over to Beowulf and his warrior crew – a special stewardship as Hrothgar made clear – Beowulf places his story about the diplomacy between peoples, the Freawaru and Ingeld match, just there where one would expect at least passing attention to how he was allowed night-time possession of the hall, in effect, of Hrothgar's 'mund.' And that, I think, is the point: he completely deflects attention to exactly how his service for Hrothgar became established. It is as though the great hall (as with the great treasures) just came into his possession as he and his men bedded down innocently for the night. Beowulf then returns to Grendel's approach and Hondscio's fate, he who was the first to fall, his body completely swallowed. The bloody-toothed slayer then thought to stuff me into a dragon-skin pouch, he adds. Thus he plays this event largely as reprisal for Hondscio's fate, rather than doing the will of the Danes, and serio-comically as resistance on his part to being devilishly wronged, shamed, and thus ignominiously treated. Of course Grendel's expectations will be reversed comically. Beowulf slips over the details of their immense struggle, saying that Grendel fled while leaving his hand in Heorot. In the following celebration the Scylding lord gave gold and treasures for that murderous onslaught while, during significant moments, breaking out in sad songs – true and sorrowful. Thus Beowulf characterizes Hrothgar as honourably generous and also, implicitly, as out of his time, as nostalgic perhaps but certainly as unlikely to achieve new arrangements in the future or new settlements. This is another way of saying that Hrothgar has not turned me, Beowulf, to himself.

Concerning the monster mother's attack and his underwater reprisal, Beowulf makes it seem that only after the second victory does Hrothgar give him the great, dynastic treasures he will soon render up to Hygelac, in exactly the same order in which he received them. He notes, falsely, that Hrothgar would have Beowulf tell Hygelac about the provenance of the splendid battle gear now in Beowulf's possession but that he should first convey Hrothgar's good favour: 'Me ðis hildesceorp Hroðgar sealed, / snotra fengel; sume worde het, / þæt ic his ærest ðe est gesægde; / cwæð þæt hyt hæfde Hiorogar cyning / leod Scyldunga lange hwile; / no ðy ær suna sinum syllan wolde, / hwatum Heorowearde, þeah he him hold wære, / breostgewaedu. Bruc ealles well!' (ll. 2155–62). It came from Heorogar who would not leave it to his son; somehow it came into Hrothgar's possession and now will go to Hygelac. When Beowulf says 'Use all well' he essentially enjoins Hygelac formally in an ambiguous gesture. He could be saying this for himself alone or on Hrothgar's behalf, as though Hrothgar would formally confer the battle-dress upon Hygelac in a gesture of alliance. Implicitly, Beowulf has Hrothgar saying here, in a parallel gesture, that he would rather give those war trappings to Beowulf (and further implicitly to Hygelac) than to his own first born. Thus in a brilliant rearrangement of details, along with invented, indirect discourse, Beowulf turns a strong adoption gesture and effort at recruitment into a combination of the disinterestedly generous giving of gold and treasures after the first fight and a quasi-diplomatic move after the second, as though Hrothgar would through Beowulf ally himself politically and militarily with *Hygelac* and the Geats, not recruit Beowulf, and as though the great alliance between Danes and Geats that Hrothgar establishes with Beowulf has nothing to do with Beowulf's initial move toward Hrothgar, his promise of aid should Hrothgar need spears against terrifying neighbours – a point Beowulf does not rehearse for Hygelac.

Beowulf brings this part of his account to a close before ordering the presentation of Hrothgar's dynastic treasures and war gear to Hygelac, all those that Hrothgar gave him with, as he insists, no strings attached; he gave him those goods unto his own keeping or judgment. Those same goods, Beowulf says to Hygelac, 'I render unto you, with favour bestow in good will, my warrior king. Still, yet furthermore is all dependent upon your kinship kindness, favour and joy (expanding the range for 'lissa'). I little have, my great kinsman, except, Hygelac, you.'

This powerful, dense, formal profession of kinship amity and loyalty is exactly what Hygelac wants to hear, what he has been *eager* to know. After all, Beowulf did depart despite the ways in which Hygelac implored him to leave Grendel to the Danes. But now he can be sure that Beowulf is deeply loyal both in word, narrative, and nature. Now Beowulf has fully returned; now he is Hygelac's Beowulf again, this immensely powerful, beloved nephew and retainer. After the great treasures are brought out and bestowed upon Hygelac and Hygd, Hygelac's return gesture is to invest Beowulf with Hrethel's splendid, unsurpassed sword, vast land holdings and a gift-seat, thus a fully endowed and established sub-kingship – Hygelac's way of saying great thanks and of transforming his relationship with his nephew into one of high power and mutual love.

The pacing-guests are guests no more, having been embraced and elevated – the retinue now of a powerful co-king, although Hygelac's domain is broader in that he is the more illustrious ('þam ðær selra wæs,' l. 2199b). On that note the scene ends, with something like a double-kingship having been established. Hygelac's endowing gratefulness while he is still active has now incarnated the Danish model of kingship, albeit through vigorous uncle and sister's-son rather than through vigorous father and son. But the Geats will be unable to reincarnate it again in Beowulf's generation, despite Hygelac having had a son by Hygd. In terms of the Danish model the Geats are cursed: Hrethel seemingly has done well, producing warrior sons. But one accidently kills the oldest and Hrethel pines away. Then Haethcyn and Hygelac are left, with Haethcyn dying in the course of avenging Swedish attacks upon Geats. Hygelac assumes the throne. After his death, Hygd offers the kingly seat to Beowulf, who turns it down in favour of Hygelac's young son, but who in turn is killed when Swedes attack him for harbouring Onela's rebellious nephews, which, finally, brings Beowulf to the throne and the beginning of his fifty-year, childless reign – until the dragon comes.

CHAPTER FIVE

The Dragon's Arrival and Beowulf's Two Departures: Deep Luck Runs Out

As many have noted, the energy and narrative complexity of the poem's second part contrasts notably with its first, seeming to go downhill. The lament of the last survivor tonally initiates an elegiac mood, a swirling theme of sad entropy. In fact the narrative pulse is nearly the opposite of that in the poem's opening, where prosperity and dynastic mastery grow before the advent of a terrible ghoul – a creature who eventually meets his nemesis, with hall and land purged of his and then his mother's pollution. This time, however, there is no establishing of succession and then a splendid departure (Scyld's) before the terrible arrival of a horrible guest. As with Grendel's initial raid, the enflamed arrival of the dragon-gæst, unanticipated, carries no tension – only destruction and a darkening of mood.

How, Beowulf wonders, has he offended God? Thoughts of kingship somehow unsecured into the future because he lacks a martial heir, a son, do not occur to him or to the poet – although later Beowulf will in his dying moments regret that he has no son out of his body, 'a guardian of heritage' ('ænig yrfeweard,' l. 2731a), to whom he could leave his battle gear. That regret is connotatively mournful in the moment: elsewhere the old father laments the death of his hanged son, not caring to wait for another 'guardian of heritage.' The dragon, although it has not simply come, comes wrathfully following a material trail, the movement of one of its treasures from its barrow into Beowulf's sitting possession. The dragon is a very bad event in the life of a good king, who could not have anticipated its arrival and who broods momentarily over the devastation it brings. What to do? Should he await a second arrival and attempt to kill the dragon as it flies, flaming, over what is left of his fortified town? No, that might be weak, one would think. Instead he departs angrily, having had an iron-covered shield fashioned, to greet the terror-guest and, he hopes, end its reign. Before that, however, we have the elegiac departure, as it were, of an entire tribe of people, voiced through its last remnant. The dragon has guarded treasure thoughtfully hidden away a long time ago, in its 'earth-house,' the weapons, plates, goblets, and ornaments of men. Whoever hid the great treasure did it carefully, thoughtfully ('þanchygende þær gehydde,' l. 2235), as though to preserve it for some future. For awhile, the burying survivor guards the treasure, mourning his friends, knowing that he likewise will have little time to make use of it. This sense of death, of fate perhaps, will appear again when Beowulf sits down before rising to challenge the dragon. Thus just here the last survivor passage sets a tone and indicates a possible way to die with the wealth of one's people, a likely counterpoint to Beowulf's sense of his crucial role between his retainers and the dragon.

Unlike the lament inclined mind, Beowulf's resolves upon battle. The so-called last survivor has lamented that those taken in battle no longer can possess or wear swords, or polish the drinking vessel; even the helmets and armour once had life in battle and now will decay much as their owners have; active men enjoying life in the hall have gone, as has their activity: the flight of the hawk, the stamping of horses, the joy, the entertaining sport of the harp. Indeed in this second part of the poem there is no harp playing, no hawking, no racing of horses, no tales in the hall as a part of feasting or celebration. However, there is speech in this part of the poem, some of it rousing and occasionally wise, and there is movement – the movement of armour, swords, and shields within the aura of grim, impending warfare. Beowulf has an alternative to the prison of lament, to lingering unto death, when he turns his troubled thoughts, his brooding and grief into martial courage, then steels himself and angrily challenges the dragon; Wiglaf also has an alternative, seizing it when he joins his lord in the fiery arena.

After the dragon's attack, Beowulf leaves his compound and his burned hall; swollen with anger ('torne gebolgen,' l. 2401b) he takes eleven retainers with him, as well as the thief who stole a cup from the dragon's hoard. Quite reluctantly, the thief shows the way to the earth-hall, the dragon's mound filled with ornamented works of metal and gold treasures. The prospect of such wealth is simply fact, not yet dwelled upon, for it is held by a terrible guardian. The poet tells us that entering there is no easy matter for any man – apparently a point

Beowulf shares, for as soon as he arrives he sits down on the headland, this gold-lord of the Geats ('goldwine Geata,' l. 2419a), and salutes his hearth-companions, wishing them luck and prosperity ('þenden hælo abead heorðgeneatum,' l. 2418). His mind is uncharacteristically sad, restless, thinking of slaughter. Again the poet expresses what Beowulf may be thinking, that his fate is exceedingly near, that fate will seek him and sunder life from body ('wyrd ungemete ... sundur gedælan / lif wið lice,' ll. 2420b–2423a). Still, Beowulf has prepared for this encounter by having an iron shield fashioned; he knows the dragon is incendiary and guards a treasure hoard, and he has brought a retinue with him, to whom he now feels moved to speak. Why?

The issue of 'luck' has come up and apparently Beowulf has made a decision. Arriving at the site enraged himself, he soon has other thoughts. Entering the barrow will be dangerous in the extreme. Moreover, what he owes his warrior-companions, who have so far *willingly* accompanied him, unlike the thief, is an explanation and perhaps some dilation on what constitutes luck and good fortune in this world he has long survived. If he feels somehow doomed himself – although not knowing just how and exactly when life will leave body – he might want better luck or at least different luck for his hearth-companions (whom he has never slain and whose successors at poem's end mourn their lord: 'Swa begnornodon Geata leode / hlafordes (hry)re, heorð-geneatas' ll. 3178–9).

And so Beowulf begins his recital of what in the way of battle he has survived since his youth. Few readers comment in any detail on this long narration. Edward B. Irving, Jr, is an exception when he devotes considerable space to Beowulf's speech as 'a new regrouping of his thoughts and faculties, a new redirection of his stored energy and will. What gives unity to the speech is a tense incompatibility ... between *sibbe* (love, security, kinship, the world of peace) and *nið* (violent battle-action), an incompatibility that is resolved ... only in the person of Beowulf himself, first through the vengeance he takes, out of his deep love, for Hygelac's death, and second through his behaviour in the present situation where he stands alone to face the dragon before the witnessing people he loves so well, better than they love him.[1] Certainly he cares for his picked retainers greatly, as I indicate below, but he would keep them safe and they are not all the people. There are other Geats and there are those who have gone, his dear kinsmen whom fate has swept away.

The main body of his account will tell of the battle storms he survived, together amounting to most of his young warrior's life, a time of war ('orleghwil'). The entire speech consumes eighty-five lines as he takes us and his retainers through some bad times and sad stories, beginning when he was seven years old, newly fostered by Hrethel, his mother's father. Hrethel gave him treasure and banquet food, mindful of kinship. That note of kinship amity is important. He then recalls how one of Hrethel's three sons accidentally killed a brother and of how Hrethel grieved, unable to avenge that death – much as a father cannot avenge the hanging of a criminal son (legally there can be no feud within the family; nor can one legally avenge the death of a criminal). Hrethel sorrowed so much that he eventually died, leaving man's joys and choosing God's light, but passing his land and city, Beowulf gnomically adds, as happy, prosperous men do, on to his off-spring, which perhaps includes the fostered Beowulf and other retainers ('eaferum laefde,' l. 2470a). At this point in his family reminiscences, Beowulf is still young and now has two uncles left, his mother's brothers Haethcyn and Hygelac, the latter of whom he has already strongly identified as his lord. That he emphasizes family, losses, and griefs therein suggests a lonely mood on his part: unlike Hrethel, he has no close kin, no family left on the maternal side, no vigorous sons and extended retainer family, other than the ones he brings with him, who might inherit his holdings and wealth.

The next set of losses he recalls follows Hrethel's death when turbulent Swedes, Ongentheow's sons, ambush and slaughter an unspecified number of Geats. That was wrongful, ciminal strife ('synn ond sacu') of a sort the poem earlier identified with Grendel's refusal to settle his feud with the Danes. Beowulf says that his kinsmen, that is, his maternal uncles avenged that feud and crime, although Haethcyn died at Ravenswood, at Ongentheow's hands, who in turn died, killed by one of Hygelac's champions, Eofor, to whom Hygelac out of gratitude gave his daughter in marriage. New family bonds follow family tragedies.

In time Beowulf develops into a mighty warrior serving his remaining uncle and lord, Hygelac. Invoking the many treasures he has from Hygelac, Beowulf says he repaid them, yielding up payment in the currency of battle, as was granted to him with his gleaming sword – thus continuing the motif of luck. In turn Hygelac gave him lands ('geald æt guðe, swa me gifeðe wæs / leohtan sweorden; he me lond forgeaf,' ll. 2491–2). Hygelac, Beowulf adds in an understatement, had no need to recruit worse champions from among the Gifthas, the Swedes or the Spear-Danes. Beowulf now is in a fighting state of mind, having passed through the sadness of family loss and unavengable deaths when he was quite young. But as he matured, 'luck,' in the form of something granted by fate ('gifeðe'), was with him. He went with Hygelac on various expeditions and raids, always out front as superb point warrior, which is why he could not prevent his dear Hygelac's death when Daeghrefn and his war band apparently cornered Hygelac and killed him. However, Beowulf, no doubt like a grief-enraged, Northern Achilles, avenged that death, physically. Daeghrefn, the Dugan champion, did not enjoy the treasure, the great neck ring, he took from Hygelac. There, under his own standard, Beowulf killed him, but not by the sword; rather, bare-handedly. Beowulf overwhelmed that champion's heart by pulverizing his ribcage. For Beowulf, the strongest of men in those days of this life, grief becomes fierce battle-rage once again. His recollection of singular bone-crushing brings Beowulf to the present moment, to the dire prospect of engaging the dragon. 'Now the sword's edge' – which he did not use on Daeghrefn – must come into play, must fight or perhaps 'warrior' for the treasure hoard ('ymb hord wigan,' l. 2509b). And so, even now he concludes, he will perform a great deed, if the dragon will come out of its earthen-hall.

To what purpose, other than providing personal exposition we have not had before and other than moving past his uncustomary gloominess of mind, thus steeling himself for combat against a creaturely inferno, does Beowulf speak here to hearth-retainers he respects (having brought them along and having already wished them luck)? We too often in reading this great poem obscure our sense of passages like this and of the scene we are in because we know, from prior reading, about some outcome: in this case that all but one of Beowulf's retainers will fail him when he most needs help against the flame throwing dragon. The retainers have not yet done anything to lose Beowulf's confidence in them. Indeed, he has both their welfare and his sense of duty close to heart. After greeting each of the 'valiant helmet bearers' for the last time, his own, 'dear retainers' ('swæse gesiðas' and perhaps thought of here as an extended family through the kinship of the hall), Beowulf, saying he is brave of mind, proposes seeking the dragon while wishing he could grip it directly, as he did long ago with Grendel. He then says this to his helmeted retainers: 'Gebide ge on beorge, byrnum werede, / secgas on searwum, hwæðer sel mæge / æfter wælræse wunde gedygan / uncer twega. Nis þæt eower sið, / ne gemet mannes, nefne min anes / þæt he wið aglæcan eofoðo dæle / eorlscype efne. Ic mid elne sceall / gold gegangan, oððe guð nimeð, / feorhbealu frecne, frean eowerne!' (ll. 2529–37).

He would have them abide on the barrow, essentially protected by their armour, and see which of the two – he or the dragon – after the rush of battle-slaughter can survive their wounds. Apparently they will be above him, looking down into what will be a terrible rush of war. For the first time in all of his adventures and campaigns, he anticipates battle so severe that he assumes he will, at the least, be wounded. He would keep his dear retainers safe from that expectation. So that when he says he will either retrieve the dragon's gold or battle will take him, *their* lord, he poses stark, battlefield alternatives. In 'niman' we have a kind of bad battle-luck or mischance, a seizing or even a robbery of life against a horribly formidable foe. He hopes for better luck in better circumstances for his warrior companions, who, he trusts, see him as their dear lord just as he thinks of them as his dear retainers. He does not, then, quite walk toward the barrow's fiery entrance because he loves his people; rather this seriously disturbing turn of luck is his alone – to face it boldly is *his* choice, much as Hrethel, although out of hopeless grief, chose 'God's light.' He does not move beyond community here so much as move out for past family and current community, in hope of better luck for his retainers than he seems to have here drawn for himself.[2] But before we close on the engagement, we need to consider a major account of what has to other scholars seemed a stylistic disappointment in the second part of the poem.

Robert Bjork admirably and comprehensively describes on several registers – rhetorical, prosodic, and sententious – a marked shift in style between the first part of the poem and the second, the part in which Beowulf speaks as he has to his retainers, although Bjork thinks the poem is not clear as to whether the entire passage in fact is addressed to those retainers. He especially notes a 'generative straddling' in which elements in speeches appear nearby in the narrative, a feature that 'conspires with other features of part two, such as the namelessness of speakers, the interrupted speeches, and the intrusion of narrative voice into speech, to erode the distinction between the poem's narrative and the spoken word.'[3] This 'erosion' seemingly is part of a general, deliberate shift that suggests a movement from a high degree of order – as expressed in rhetorically complex and balanced speech, in exchanges of speech and in courtly ritual – to a chaos largely reflected in the bleeding of narrative into speech, in interruptions of speech and in a perceived ineffectuality of speech. Presumably the latter is the case in Wiglaf's speech to the assembled, remaining

Geat nobility who have come to the sad scene of parallel corpses, Beowulf and the dragon.

True, on the namelessness of speakers, we do not know the messenger's name nor do we know the name of the mourning woman near poem's end (her worries being obscured by the nearly total erasure of a key line). Moreover, we do not know the names of the warriors riding around Beowulf's funeral pyre. But that may be how such matters are supposed to be narrated in heroic story: we do not know the names of Scyld's dear mourners either or of the many warriors other than Hengest on the funeral pyre in the Finnsburg episode; there we do not even know Hildeburh's son's name, Hengest's nephew. A kind of grievous anonymity characterizes funerals in the poem. Moreover, functionaries do not always have names, as in the cases of the coast watch and the warriors assigned to guard Beowulf's ship in part one. There is no clear reason, then, why Wiglaf's messenger should have a name in that he largely speaks on Wiglaf's behalf. That his speech, like Beowulf's, occasions no return speech is an interesting fact in this section of the poem: speeches themselves have become narratives more than crafted appeals or responses to challenges or situations. Indeed, that alteration of speech into narrative can account for nearly all of the stylistic shifts Bjork gathers together for us. Yet even here there is a surprise: the speeches are either caring, or concern community (if only the end of community in the lament of the last survivor burying armour and treasures). And Wiglaf himself is a forceful surprise, given to speak eloquently and in maxims as he effectively reorganizes the Geats (see below).

So, Beowulf has spoken to and saluted his dear retainers. He now turns to the dreadful confrontation before him. In the first half of the unfolding event, Beowulf angrily calls out the dragon because he dare not engage its flame-encompassed entry way – even the stream issuing from the barrow is on fire. As the two meet in mutual hatred, swollen rage, and fear, Beowulf reluctantly steps backward in the face of the dragon's onslaught, his great sword breaking into pieces as he strikes the dragon's armour-like bone. Beowulf, surrounded by dragon fire, is anguished, his breathing laboured. At this point his dear retainers might rally around him, despite having been told to stay out of the fight, to watch only from a safe place, protected by distance, height and their armour. Beowulf's near-mortal suffering now trumps his clearly stated and doubly-defined challenge earlier – that this turn of luck is his alone and that he has, alone, survived great battles, done glorious things. Seeing their lord suffer the dragon's heat and flames, perhaps panicked by the sudden, thunderous conflagration, his retainers flee to the woods. However, once there one of them has better surging of thought. Leaving the relative safety of the woods to help would be a gift of magnanimity understood by the poet as the triumph of true kinship: 'sibb' æfre ne mæg / wiht onwendan þam ðe wel þenceð' (ll. 2600b–2601). That one retainer in fact steps forward to help is to his great credit; Wiglaf notes that in exchange for the treasures and weapons Beowulf gave them they had all vowed to help in battle should *need* arise (both occasion and ethical call). Their brave commitment is why he chose them in the first place, accounting them good spear-warriors; and although he thought to perform this brave deed alone, because he has performed many deeds of glory, deeds of audacious vows and daring (the oddly phrased 'dæda dollicra,' l. 2646a) – Wiglaf has understood this much in Beowulf's apologia – now the time has come that he needs the strength and support of good battle-warriors.[4] Wiglaf says he would rather have the dragon's flames embrace his body along with his gold-giver's than leave Beowulf to die alone; he thinks it unfitting that they bear their shields back without having killed the enemy and defended Beowulf's life, the life of the lord of the Weders.

All of what he says is most commendable, speaking as it does to Wiglaf's loyalty, sense of honour and generosity. In effect, his aid is a free gift given that Beowulf has told them all to stay put, safely out of harm's way. That the other ten do just that is not completely to their shame (although they do eventually emerge feeling ashamed), despite what Wiglaf says to them when they show up after Beowulf and the dragon are dead. Beowulf in fact never mentions the other ten in his exchanges with Wiglaf when the two manage to kill the dragon after the dragon lethally, poisonously bites Beowulf on the shoulder. Beowulf focuses entirely on Wiglaf, calling him beloved and urging him to retrieve treasures so that he can gaze on them before he dies; in effect, he thinks of the treasure as his man price for his people. Wiglaf departs within that part of the scene, eventually returning with a huge armload of glittering treasures.

In that return he finds Beowulf still alive. Beowulf gives thanks for the sight of the treasures and notes that he has little time to live; yet he is pleased that the hoard of treasures is there, something he has gained for the sake of his people. He urges Wiglaf to attend to the needs of the people and to have them raise a burial mound for him after the pyre.

He then gives his beloved Wiglaf a golden neck ring, his spectacular helmet, his ring, and corselet. He would have Wiglaf 'use them well'; essentially, by those gifts and those words, Beowulf confers war-band leadership upon this last of his Waegmunding kinsmen, all of his others, on his mother's side essentially, having been swept away by fateful events; he will follow after them. Perhaps this moment would also refresh kingship for the Geats, Wiglaf having shown martial courage. It is in that altered status Beowulf confers upon him that Wiglaf will berate the other retainers – who are said sarcastically to be late for battle and are also called 'faith-beliers,' rather than the usual 'coward' by which we translate 'treologan.'[5] Something like wrongly turned thought and oath-breaking inheres in the word. When the tardy retainers approach Wiglaf, who still sadly bathes the now dead Beowulf, he ends up saying that they would be better dead than living a life of thought turned backward ('edwitlif').

Beowulf's move to call out the dragon and fight him alone, as we have seen, has been motivated by concern for the safety of his retainers as much as by a hero's turning of grief into martial rage and a hope for the luck of singular combats such as those he undertook and survived in the past. His is not a simple mood or a simple motive: in the course of his account, what I have called his apologia, he explains his decision in effect to his retainers in such a way as to minimize any sense they might have that he thinks little of them. Much as he loved and in some ways still mourns his mother's family and his dear Hygelac, he respects them greatly; they are dear to him. Yet he would undertake this dismaying peril alone, as he has so often in the past, hoping for some special luck now and because he understands it as somehow his luck alone. He feels the nearness of fate. Thus there is more here than the heroic ego and its clarion boast; indeed, that ego only arises at the point of decision, when he has roused himself to face the dragon. He would have a different luck, as I have said, in different circumstances for his retainers. That matters do not work out happily for him or for them is not the issue. Indeed how this fight works out, with Wiglaf's intervention, Beowulf's urging that Wiglaf recover some of the treasure and then his extending of war-band leadership to him – that has been quite a surprise, in the turns of events, in the good luck or not of various moments. No one could have predicted, not even Beowulf himself, just how he would die, if die he must; no one could have predicted the emergence of a hitherto unknown retainer, a Waegmunding kinsman, the young and resolute Wiglaf, Weohstan's son;

and no one could have predicted what this new leader would do first.

In the course of castigating the other retainers and predicting that they and their families – their kin ('eowrum cynne,' 2885b) – will suffer, he says that all joys and comforts and rights will end for them, that they will have to move about, deprived of all that, when nobles from afar learn about their 'flight,' their turned-wit behaviour. Wiglaf essentially exiles them for the better good of the rest of the Geats. Then he sends a messenger to those Geats who are back in the fortified enclosure. That arrival brings unhappy, unpleasant news, although the messenger's news is more devastating in one sense and less so in another than was the dragon's arrival the night before. There will be some reparative activity for the waiting nobles.

The messenger's speech has been taken almost universally as a set-piece predicting doom for the Geats once their fractious and risible neighbours, especially the Swedes and Franks, learn of Beowulf's death. Yet the speech has a social context beyond the implied call to arms Edward B. Irving suggests:[6] Wiglaf has to take command; he is young, having just survived his first, serious combat, and thus is probably not well known to the group of nobles among the Geats – the 'eorlweorod' (l. 2893b), who sit sad-minded with their shields, back from the edge of the cliff, expecting either the end of days for their beloved lord or his return. The only other time Geats sit like this is fifty years in the past, among the Danes beside the mere into which Beowulf had some hours before disappeared from view. When they see gore welling up eventually, Beowulf's retainers then desire but do not expect to see their friendly lord again; nevertheless they stay while the Danes leave for Heorot, thinking that the mere-wolf has cut Beowulf down (ll. 1599–1605). Fifty years ago Beowulf returned to his warriors; this time he does not and the news comes through a human voice, not the emergence of hero and bloody trophies. Wiglaf has commanded. He is now in some sense in this time the leader of these nobles, who need to know quickly what has happened – that the 'joy-giver,' the lord of the Geats lies on a bed of slaughter, dead from the dragon's doing, who lies dead also, sick from seax-wounds. Also they need to know that Wiglaf, Weohstan's son and a noble, sits there over Beowulf, one nobleman over another. Weary of mind he keeps watch over the dead, over both the beloved and the loathed (the dragon). So Wiglaf is singled out here, made important in this grim scene. The other retainers, the ten and their kin whom Wiglaf has in effect exiled, are not mentioned.

Then the messenger opens his word hoard of dire expectations about what will happen once news of Beowulf's death reaches Swedes and Frisians, given feuds in the past between the Geats and each of those peoples. He reprises Hygelac's ill-fated raid among the Frisians as well as the bloody events that culminated at Ravenswood between Hygelac's Geats and Ongentheow. Somehow what the messenger has to explain is great mortality and the vulnerability of a battle king's people after his death. The poem may also here reflect the poet's expansive sense of doom hanging over the unhappy events of the dragon fight, the sad history of the dragon's treasure, and the likely aftermath. Clearly elegy, sadness, and terrible prescience affect the tonalities of several speeches, here and elsewhere in this section of the poem. A kind of unanswerably sad monologism seems to characterize the last third of *Beowulf*, at least if we mainly focus on the long passages of speech to silent audiences.[7] But of course the Geat nobles do not need to hear the messenger's speech.

What he tells them must be background they already know, his anticipations then going without saying. Even the poem's listener or reader can before this expect much of what the messenger anticipates. For both the poet and Beowulf have noted Hygelac's ill-fated adventure among the Frisians, for different reasons; and Beowulf has given us indication already that the death of a king brings trouble from turbulent neighbours in his account of Swedish ambushes after Hrethel died. Therefore the messenger's rehearsals must have some other social function and motive in the poem's narrative pulse. In effect, I would say, they bind these sad-minded nobles to the probably even sadder Wiglaf; Beowulf has not returned; but Wiglaf will – or better, the nobles will go to Wiglaf as though to their lord of distress, which the messenger tells them to do as he sketches out features of the funeral pyre and the likelihood of hard times ahead. On many cold dawns they perforce will raise their spears as the black raven awakens them, the raven who circles above doomed men, regaling the eagle with tales of how he and the wolf stripped flesh from the slaughtered. The messenger courageously projects these hateful images, unblinkingly. It is that courage that deepens the link between the nobles and Wiglaf, Weohstan's son, although nothing the messenger says predicts the Geats' utter demise – indeed, they have to be alive and armed to grasp their spears on those cold, dire mornings.

They rise and depart, going swollen-teared to the headland to see that doleful wonder, their incomparable lord lying dead on the sand; they also see the strange, ghastly sight of the dead dragon, stretched out to its fifty-foot length. But they have not come to gaze only at a grievous sideshow. They have come to bear Beowulf home as well, to his funeral pyre: for that, however, they need to heed Wiglaf, insistently called Weohstan's son to separate him from the many Geatish nobles, as well as, I believe, to indicate that he is not close kin, as a sister's son, for example, to Beowulf. He is part Swedish, as was Beowulf's father; so Beowulf is of the mysterious Waegmundings perhaps through a grandmother.[8] Wiglaf, however, has garnered epithets in the course of the dragon slaying and the immediate aftermath: he is battle-brave and he is wise (ll. 3111a; 3120a). It is as 'se wisa' that he chooses the seven best nobles to go with him into the dragon's barrow and begin bringing out the great treasures. Having already gone into the barrow and returned, he is their guide at least and their guarantee that the curse on the treasure has been lifted. But as he commands and chooses he is their leader in every sense of the word, although not called a gold-giver or a people's guardian. First, however, he needs to establish himself and who they are in relation to their glorious king now dead. What should they think?

Wiglaf begins gnomically: 'Oft sceall eorl monig anes willan / wræc adreog*an*, swa us geworden is' (ll. 3077–8). This sounds like the beginning of a reformative proposal: often many nobles, because of the will of one, suffer, as with us has become the case, is the case. The 'us' in this context can only be Wiglaf and the nobles who have now joined him to view Beowulf's corpse and the dragon's. Seamlessly, Wiglaf has identified himself with them and them with him, while seeming to set their plight as an outcome of something like high wilfulness or tyranny on the part of one person, in this case Beowulf.

His remark presages revolt or at least a reformation. Wiglaf continues: 'we could not convince our beloved lord, by any means, not to greet that gold-guardian, the dragon; we could not convince him to let the beast lie dormant, where he has long been, until the world ends. Instead, he held to his high fate;' the hoard has been opened at terrible cost: 'wæs þæt gifeðe to swið, / þe ðone [þeodcyning] þyder ontyhte' (ll. 3085b–3086). Although substituting 'fate' for 'strife,' line 3085b otherwise replays the devastating effect of Grendel's initial depredations in Heorot, the too strong strife he brought being 'hateful and long lasting' (ll. 191b–192a). Here Wiglaf may remember Beowulf's emphasis on luck and on what fate does or does not give – in this case it both drew and incited Beowulf thither, to combat with the dragon. But the hoard has been opened, the 'possessor's' favour received, however mixed that favour – involving the lifting of a binding curse – has proven to be (see the difficulties of 'agendes est,' ll. 3070–5).

That implicit blame and then exculpation of Beowulf accomplishes two things not previously attempted. None of Beowulf's retainers tried to persuade him, not in the hall and not on the headland outside the dragon's barrow. Rather, now, Wiglaf would draw in the remaining nobles in this fiction of attempted restraint and callow advice. Of course the dragon would come again to fly in its night joy, as evidenced by the continuing flames issuing from its barrow. Beowulf's decision to forge the shield and challenge the dragon, given the large-scale destruction of his compound, the surrounding lands, and his hall was locally the right one, although its long-term implications, given the outcome, are troubling. Indeed, the dragon incinerated the best of halls, the gift-seat of the Geats (l. 2327a) and so perhaps dear Hygelac's hall before becoming Beowulf's own (if so Beowulf's enraged grief over Hygelac's death so long ago might have been revived here, in a second death, so to speak, and added to his own loss). The Geats will have to move frequently, defending themselves against early dawn raids that take their toll. Wiglaf here raises the fiction of counsel, of something he and the remaining nobles attempted but which of course they did not. The upshot of this is simultaneously to separate Beowulf from them as a hero holding to his 'high destiny' and to unite them in their modest, pragmatic wisdom and hope (that the dragon would stay in its den until doomsday).

Wiglaf's claims also reflect a universal about grief: we blame the dead even as we know that neither they nor we could have acted otherwise, whatever we assert about our lesser actions and advice. This, as one of the effects of great mortality, may be especially the case with larger than life heroes.[9] At the immediate level, however, Wiglaf's remarks work up to praise of Beowulf and then to a series of actions, to which Wiglaf would exhort the Geats ('Uton nu efstan,' l. 3101a). First, however, Wiglaf needs to establish himself as Beowulf's executor. He says that he went into the dragon's mound and brought out rich hoard-treasures, a great burden ('mægenbyrðenne,' l. 3091b), the half-line compound occurring elsewhere only to characterize Beowulf's recovery from Grendel's lair of the monster's head and the great sword hilt (l. 1625a). This parallel is arresting in that Grendel's huge head marks the definitive end of that source of terror and the great sword hilt contains a text of the flood, of ancient strife, divine requital, and the death of giants. Now the great burden is dragon's gold buried by a last survivor and then cursed, the curse having been lifted. Brought to Beowulf that gold signifies his man price, as we have already noted, and is something he would pass on to his people. For Wiglaf it is something he bears in his hands to his still living king, who is wise and still perceptive ('wis ond gewittig,' l. 3094a). By these terms Wiglaf authenticates the validity of Beowulf's wishes, who spoke of many things. Old and sorrowful ('gomol on gehðo') Beowulf, Wiglaf says, urged me to greet you, requesting that, because of your friendly lord's deeds – thus legitimizing his commands through Beowulf's legacy of generosity – that you build a large and famous mound for him on the place of the funeral pyre, given that he was among men on this wide earth the worthiest of warriors for as long as he was able to make use of his treasures.

Presumably that praise of Beowulf's honour and worth is Wiglaf's, who omits Beowulf's imperative that he, Wiglaf, use the treasure to look after the Geats. Thus it would seem that Wiglaf implicitly wants the treasure already piled near Beowulf joined with more, which they will soon enter the barrow to extract. The whole store then will be part of Beowulf's funeral and the erection of his great mound. At least that is how the Geats will in fact handle the treasures after the sighting and recovery of them, to which Wiglaf now urges them, he leading them at least as Beowulf's executor (they are still operating in relation to Beowulf). He then orders others to prepare a bier so that when they emerge from the dragon's barrow they can carry their beloved lord to where he will long abide in the Wielder's keeping. After, in his role as a brave battle-warrior ('hæle hildedior,' l. 3111a), he would have them announce to many warriors, to all who own dwellings, that men of property are to bring wood for the funeral pyre. This is not quite a requisition; rather his command is a mobilization of the goods and retinues needed to inter their beloved king properly.

What Wiglaf has done in a series of assertions about Beowulf and related commands is worth noting step by step. The nobles who have come with the messenger presumably are too stunned and sorrowful to do more than abstractly know what they should do. With Beowulf's clarity and authority behind him, Wiglaf takes charge and marshals the Geats' resources and strength. He even produces something like a bittersweet but eloquent lament for the still to be cremated and interred Beowulf: 'Now fire shall consume the strong-man of warriors, he who often experienced the shower of iron, who with strength pressed on through the storm of arrows over the shield wall, [where] shafts did their duty; feathered gear eager for death supported the arrow head.' That eloquence befits his raised status: although hand-maimed by dragon fire, he is a powerful warrior wise in words and deeds (*gravitas* and *celeritas*).

Wiglaf, honoured and elevated at just this point as 'se snotra sunu Wihstanes,' then chooses the seven best of the king's remaining thanes to follow quickly his lead into the barrow; this is now a retinue of the very brave going, with wise Wiglaf their light-bearing leader, into the forbidding underworld of dragon possession. Quickly they all go down and plunder the hoard, returning to the outside, where they push the dragon corpse over the cliff into the sea, load all of the countless, twisted gold treasures into a wagon and carry Beowulf to his final resting place at Whale's Headland. Presumably Wiglaf is with them through all of this, experienced as he is both in entering the dragon's barrow and exiting with an enormous armful of treasure. But we do not hear from, or of, him again as the Geats in their mournful plurality turn to the funeral obsequies for their great, superlative lord, last described as 'har hilde[rinc],' the hoary, grey-haired warrior.

Still, in this last leave-taking or departure scene there is a final, superb surprise. What will the mourning Geats say about their famous, glorious, and beloved lord ('mære þeoden'; 'hlaford leof'), whose funeral smoke rises auspiciously? We might expect gestures similar to those of the Danes long ago when sending the terrifyingly military Scyld out to sea, richly honoured by treasures and a golden banner. And indeed the Geats do consign helmets, shields, and shining chain mail to Beowulf's pyre, as he apparently requested. But while those Danes more than five generations ago, and early in the lineation of the poem, are sad when they produce Scyld's ship burial, they say nothing the poet cares to report. Nor, in the Finnsburg funeral, do we know even indirectly what Hildeburh says as she lyrically mourns her kinsmen. Now, however, we are told in generalizations what the great nobles said in their riding around Beowulf's funeral mound, his ashes and the dragon's treasures interred therein: 'cwædon þæt he wære wyruldcyning[a] / manna mildust ond mon(ðw)ærust, / leodum liðost ond lofgeornost' (ll. 3180–2). The conventional anonymity of funereal grief has here been lifted into a report about what was fitting, praise-worthy and superlative in the thoughts of the Geats.

The phrase 'manna mildust' has beguiled generations of translators into supposing that the Geats here are said to praise Beowulf as superlatively 'mild.' It is a gift to all scholars and readers of the poem to have, instead, Seamus Heaney's beautiful and provocative 'they said that of all the kings upon the earth / he was the man most gracious and fair-minded, / kindest to his people and keenest to win fame.'[10] Yet that gift – a rendering of Beowulf's graciousness – is not quite enough: for Beowulf's Geats actually are said to call him the most *generous* of men. In fact 'milts' is glossed by Klaeber as 'kindness,' not mildness, and 'kindness' in a great battle king essentially is generosity within the war band. Looking at the other superlatives, we find the last, 'lofgeornost,' also from the register of the comitatus, whereas one of the middle two – Heaney's 'kindest' – actually comes from the register of kinship amity, a register Wealhtheow uses when she urges the young and superbly successful Beowulf to befriend her sons, not as their would-be lord, but as a kind of kinsman: 'ond þyssum cnyhtum wes / lara liðe ... Beo þu suna minum / dædum gedefe' (ll. 1219b–1227a). In 'lara liðe' she would have Beowulf instruct them kindly; in 'dædum gedefe' she would have him be fittingly gentle, thus reinforcing the kinship realm in her meaning. The fourth term, 'monðwære' echoes in her part claim, part command that here in Heorot each noble is to the other mild of mind and reciprocally loyal while being loyal vertically altogether to their lord, Hrothgar: 'þegnas syndon geþwære' (l. 1230b). Wealtheow very carefully picks her terms from a non-warrior register, indeed, from the realm of kin to kin amity.[11]

That the Geats would combine comitatus values with kinship ones – and even 'monðwærust' has something of kin amity to it – is astounding. Here they praise Beowulf, seeing in him virtues that expand great kingship from that of dedicated war-band leadership to that of family harmony as well, something implicit we can now see, in retrospect, in Beowulf's personal focus on losses within the family and his concern for the good luck, safety, and well-being of those retainers he took with him into the dragon's terrain. The two-generational, Danish model of kingship is here replaced, although hardly abandoned, by a comprehensively extended one as reflected in Beowulf's superlative, highly praised person. The *gravitas* of the 'sitting' king, his ethical role as lordly rewarder, receiver, rightful proposer, and disposer, has opened to include kinship amity, that is, family values. Sovereignty has expanded, perhaps even changed. The great king in that praise is not only all that he has needed to be according to the Danish model of kingship; he is now also the chief kinsman of both his *comitatus* and his people. On that astonishing note, this great poem comes to its end much as it began, with a royal funeral – a ship funeral then, a cremation now. In between, as I have shown, the variable pulse of arrival and departure scenes has galvanized a highly dramatic, narrative poem about heroic tensions, surprises, hopes, and joys, then sorrows, joys, and sorrows again.

Conclusion

Clearly the poet looks back to a much earlier time, while in past tense perspective bringing that world forward toward his own – a world we know historically as institutionally more complex, especially given church and clergy, king and court; it was socially stratified for different levels of nobility and landholdings, included slavery, and was economically organized for both mundane and prestige trade (with coinage, emporia, and mints). Moreover, in Alfred's day, through a well-framed law code, even if its sometimes random contents often only gesture toward completeness, and also through an educational program for great men, the king's administration is extended and military service and logistics reorganized, along with the establishing of a system of fortified places throughout Wessex and Mercia (which in turn further enhance royal control).

However, law code fines and punishments, military organization in general and those fortified places especially tell us that Wessex and Mercia and other Ango-Saxon kingdoms are in a world of sometimes hostile arrivals and departures, of ætheling tensions and assassinations, of the ascensions and deaths or even the killing of kings, of temporary, often hard won peace and nightmarish incursions from the sea if not from marsh and mere. Perhaps the narrative pulse of *Beowulf* courses strong from the times of Offa, Alfred, and beyond insofar as the poem might be taken by Anglo-Saxons as a model, for their times, of good customs, heroic, fame-enhancing behaviour and great kingship in at least two forms: the two-generational Danish model and the Beowulfian model of sovereignty enlarged to include kinship amity.

While succession issues are hardly settled before Alfred's time – almost any royal male could claim throne-worthiness – and then only fitfully after that, the two-generational model may well have been either a ninth- or tenth-century innovation or a deep model perhaps revived during Alfred's time or by his successors. Afterall, Anglo-Saxon kings, despite Bede's euphemerization of him, probably claimed descent from Woden for either sacral or charismatic reasons. Almost certainly their ancestors did. Moreover, the Scyld Scefing story is in some way linked to royal luck and to issues of fertility – if 'scef' equals 'sheaf' and Beowulf I should have been Beow or 'barley.' As set out in chapter 1 that story also, or perhaps even centrally, involves the rejuvenation of kingship itself from one of destructive arrogance and pride (as figured in Heremod) to a bipolar model of prowess and *gravitas*, with each pole alternatingly refreshed across overlapping generations. Although, we cannot expect the poetical and historical parallels to be simple mirrorings, at the least something like a functioning, two-generation model has notable military advantages: if a vigorous king and his equally vigorous, younger brother or son fight well, they can better deal with an armed threat, as Æthelred and Alfred, his younger brother, do, by dividing up their forces or combining them as the changing military situation dictates.

Moreover, the king's son, or else younger brother, can take on some of the king's martial force, thus softening the king and further foregrounding his *gravitas* – a pious aspect of which may underlie Asser's story about King Æthelred's refusal to leave mass until the priest had finished, thus causing Alfred's arrival at Ashdown ahead of him. Presumably, in turn, Alfred's son, Edward, is a vigorous, tempered combatant during the latter years of Alfred's reign, as implied in ealderman Æthelweard's account of the closing years. Also Edward's budding *gravitas* is perhaps expressed through his work as an administrator at court and through his attestations in a few charters, in one of which he is styled as *rex*.[1] The main beneficiary of lands in Alfred's will, Edward, upon becoming king, proves that he can deal forcefully with a rebellious cousin and that cousin's Danish allies, whom the cousin, Æthelwald, may have suborned. If, as Audrey L. Meany argues on stylistic and other grounds, the Scyld Scefing prologue is largely an early tenth-century addition to some version of the poem, then we might suppose a closer link than would otherwise seem likely between Christian theories of authority, lordship, and kingship in the time of Alfred, his brothers, and sons and the shaping of kingship ideals in *Beowulf*.

However idealized behaviour, values, and kingly institutions are in the poem, at least in matters of host and guest tensions, and of variously tempered arrivals and departures, *Beowulf* is a surprisingly complex drama in scene after scene, perhaps reflecting Anglo-Saxon reality more nearly than does Asser, say, in his account of King Alfred's time and rule. For Asser, Alfred is a paragon of both martial vigour and generosity, as well as hospitality and inspiration in his desire to rule well, wisely, and with an educated cohort of thanes. When Alfred summons Asser to his side, Asser says he is warmly welcomed and then soon enough earnestly asked to commit himself and become part of Alfred's household.[2] Asser hesitates, not wanting to abandon his obligations, holdings and people in Wales, but Alfred persists, hoping for at least an arrangement whereby Asser would spend half the year with him and half back home. When Asser finally commits himself to an extended stay with Alfred, he is received honorably and stays for eight months. When Alfred finally allows him to leave, he gives him gifts of monasteries and indicates that he will reward him even more handsomely at some later time. Such generosity toward a revered cleric, maker of a personal commonplace book from scripture for Alfred, and eventual biographer, might not seem unusual. But when Alfred divides his tax revenues to reward those who serve him, he sets aside cheerfully, according to Asser, a portion for 'foreigners of all races who came to him from places near and far and asked money from him (or even if they did not ask), to each one according to his particular station.'[3] Moreover, he schools Edward in kindness and generosity toward countrymen and foreigners as well. This may or may not be an entirely fulsome view of Wessex's intelligent, pious, and warlike king. But it hardly gives us insight into how strangers might be received during normal times as well as during times of intense threat.

If in *The Odyssey* strangers have Zeus's protection, in Anglo-Saxon England they have the king's, expressed in various law codes. That protection reveals several things: that strangers (who may be traders) might be preyed upon because they have no local kin group to support them should they meet losses, injury, or death at someone's hands; that regularized hospitality toward a stranger effectively binds the host as protector and as accountable surety; that the stranger might for his own purposes in fact pose a danger to the kingdom or some part of it.

Consider first one of Ine's laws, capitulary 23: 'Gif mon elðeodigne ofslea, se cyning ah twædne dæl weres þriddan dæl sunu oððe mægas' ('if someone slays a foreigner, the king possess two parts of the wergild, a son or kinsmen the third part').[4] With variations covering the foreigner who has no kin or lacks kin but is under clerical protection, we see Ine providing a safeguard for travellers and traders. They certainly cannot be slain with impunity. Here Ine would enlarge the king's peace and also his own reach. When in Alfred's case laws are promulgated jointly with Guthrum, and then again between Edward and possibly some other Guthrum, we have a special, emphatic provision for the stranger, formulated in such a way as to put the stranger – in matters of loss of property or life – under at least the protection of the 'eorl' where the event occurs if the stranger has no other kinsmen, but certainly also the king's. If an offence is not promptly compensated for to Christ and king, the king of that territory shall avenge the deed very deeply ('oððe þa dæde wrece swiðe deope,' capitulary 12). This proviso probably is a response to the likelihood of movement across the Danelaw, by Vikings on the one hand and West-Saxons and others on the other. Clearly neither Alfred nor Guthrum counts on easy hospitality and an ubiquitous welcoming of travellers in either kingdom.

The Kentish laws of Hlothhere and then of Eadric state in capitulary 15 that if a man is hospitable, that is, receives and feeds for three days a trader or anyone else who comes from over the border, then that man assumes responsibility for the foreigner should he do evil or harm to somebody – a responsibility exercised either in bringing the foreigner to justice or giving compensation on his behalf. This law seems a response to the need for local protection in light of a kind of kinship and lordship created by repeated interaction with a foreigner. But in a law of Wihtred's, one of Eadric's successors, an accused foreigner ('gest') might clear himself at the altar with his own oath.

The foreigner might not come into the country intending harm; realistically, however, such harm might materialize and thus someone needs to account for the foreigner or else be prepared to hear the foreigner's oath in a sacred place. In a more threatening case, in one of Ine's laws (codicil 20), where the foreigner is travelling off the highway through the woods, and does not shout or blow his horn to indicate his presence, he is to be considered a thief, subject to being killed at will or else captured and held for ransom. Taken as a composite view of strangers over time, these capitularies from the laws of different kings suggest the danger strangers might encounter, and thus the protection they would need, the responsibilities incurred by extended hosting, and the possible evil of strangers themselves, especially those who might wander off the king's highway. Alfred even has a capitulary (34) concerning traders who would assemble men for travelling into the country: they must declare before the king's reeve the number of men they are taking and take only those men they can bring to justice if need be. Groups of men, necessarily at least lightly armed, pose an even greater threat than would a lone thief or marauder. No doubt traders were known to turn raiders – if only as cattle thieves – or suspected at times of doing so.

Where Asser portrays a most generous Alfred toward foreigners, Alfred's laws and those of other kings are here and there acknowledgments that foreigners might have other than honorable intentions. That view nicely matches the tension we see in *Beowulf* when the powerful hero arrives, unsummoned and unannounced, with his well-armed troop of warrior-sailors. Both the coast watch and Wulfgar, Hrothgar's officer, challenge the Geats to reveal themselves, to clarify what they seem to be and thus dispel the possibility that they are marauders. But in the event of being lordless, the guests or strangers – Beowulf's Geats – would in their turn need protective clarification from Hrothgar, which is what Beowulf hopes for, given that he will have died doing something heroic on Hrothgar's behalf (vengefully seeking Grendel's mother). Even the welcome arrival in Hygelac's hall is not without its pressing questions: has Beowulf, because of repeated service and rewards, and as recipient of repeated hospitality, returned now with mixed loyalties, with mixed obligations or even with some sense that he now is tied to two lords? Hygelac is intensely eager to know, as I have argued in chapter 4. Upon his own death, Beowulf would have Wiglaf look after the needs of the people, who, lordless, would likely suffer the enmity of powerful, aggrieved neighbours. As matters turn, it looks like the Geats will become strangers to their own land, obliged on cold mornings to face raids repeatedly, moving from foreign place to place – at least if one credits Wiglaf's messenger's forebodings. Perhaps in the light of these parallels, we might conclude that *Beowulf* is both a noble and powerfully realistic envisioning of an Anglo-Saxon world, however much set initially in a distant past among the deeds of terrifying kings and rapacious marsh-walkers, then brought somewhat forward to a mournful horizon of reported praise-song for Beowulf's lordly generosity, harmony-inducing, kinship-amity and eagerness for fame in those terms. At the least, it is something like that, with a dramatic, socially complex, and highly changeable pulse of variously characterized arrivals and departures, as well as secondary arrivals and departures, departures and arrivals, within larger scenes of the same.

Notes

1. The Narrative Pulse of *Beowulf*: Arrivals and Departures

1 Kathryn Hume, 'The Theme and Structure of *Beowulf*,' *Studies in Philosophy* 72 (1975), 1–27; H.L. Rogers, 'Beowulf's Three Great Fights,' *Review of English Studies* 6 (1955), 339–55. John D. Niles, Beowulf: *The Poem and Its Tradition* (Cambridge, MA, 1983), thinks of the three fights as the poem's core incidents but sees the overall structure as 'a series of major and minor pairs' moving in, so to speak, like inset diptyches one might add, on the underwater encounter with Grendel's mother and near death (pp. 158–9); Gale R. Owen-Crocker, *The Four Funerals in* Beowulf (Manchester, 2000), p. 236; J.R.R. Tolkien, '*Beowulf*: The Monsters and the Critics,' *Publications of the British Academy* 22 (1936), 245–95.

2 Some work has been done on the 'type-scene,' such as the hero-on-the-beach (David K. Crowne, 'The Hero on the Beach: An Example of Composition by Theme in Anglo-Saxon Poetry,' *Neuphilologische Mitteilungen* 61 [1960], 362–72), where certain general features or images are common. Such a form may also underlie feud stories, for example; they conform with some variation to an underlying 'type.' See Earl R. Anderson, 'Formulaic Typescene Survival: Finn, Ingeld, and Nibelungenlied,' *English Studies* 61 (1980), 293–301. In part discussion of 'type scenes' may be just discussions of genre or else of the kind of work an episode is supposed to accomplish. In no case do such discussions rise to the level of drama inherent in a scene unfolding in its own terms, given the expectations, worries and interactions of its characters and creatures, with outcomes that can be surprising. It is true that at a gross level we can see alternations of speech and event or action in *Beowulf*. All warrior arrivals and departures require speech and all are at least potentially troublesome or

else problematic actions. Theodore Andersson, 'Tradition and Design in *Beowulf*,' in *Old English Literature in Context*, ed. John D. Niles, pp. 90–106 (Cambridge, 1980), reprinted in *Interpretations of* Beowulf: *A Critical Anthology*, ed. R.D. Fulk, pp. 219–34 (Bloomington, 1991), has moved toward my sense of narrative pulse in *Beowulf* by proposing the following types of scenes in Beowulf: outdoor battle, convivial or celebratory hall scenes; battle in the hall; journeys in quest of heroic confrontation, sentinal scene, welcoming scene, sending of messenger, consultation of hero with kings or queens, flytings, and leave-taking scenes. 'These ten scene types account for most of the action in the old heroic lay ... [and in] *Beowulf*. One difference is that the *Beowulf* poet uses each type, which normally occurred just once in a heroic lay, repeatedly ... His repertory is traditional; only the scope is new' (*A Preface to the Nibelungenlied* [Stanford, 1987], p. 24). The difference Andersson notes is everything in setting up the possibility of a narrative pulse; several instances of particular types of scenes fill that pulse out variably; and the tensions of arrivals and what is at stake in departures reflect what has happened dramatically. Earlier, promising approaches to the 'rhythm' of the poem conceived it too statically in terms of a polarity of speech and action: see Vilhelm Grønbech, *Culture of the Teutons*, trans. William Worster (Oxford, 1931), where giving and receiving have great import; see also Peter Clemoes, 'Action in *Beowulf* and Our Perception of It,' in Daniel Calder, ed, *Old English Poetry* (Berkeley, 1979), pp. 147–68, where the 'interplay' of speech and action receives attention; Linda Georgiana, 'King Hrethel's Sorrow and the Limits of Heroic Action in *Beowulf*,' *Speculum* 62 (1987), 829–50, who laments the lack of attention to speeches; Robert E. Bjork, 'Speech as Gift,' *Speculum* 69 (1994), 993–1022, where speech as conversation and exchange reflects social identity and order; Andy Orchard, *A Critical Companion to* Beowulf (Cambridge, 2003), where speeches within expansive scenes appear as part of a choreography. Speech and action are central features of the poem but we miss the larger movements if we focus on speeches as set pieces, whether answered or not. Again, every human arrival and departure involves speech, if only indirect, narrative generalization about what was mourned and done by unnamed characters – as in the cases of Scyld's funeral and Beowulf's.

3 All citations are to F.R. Klaeber, ed., *Beowulf*, 3d edition (Boston, 1950).

4 Joyce Lionarons, '*Beowulf*: Myth and Monsters,' *English Studies* 77 (1996), 1–14, canvasses all the uses of 'guest' and 'ghastly spirit' in the poem, focusing on the way in which guest and host relationships can be reversed and the elaborate ways in which the monster-guest theme

works in all three fights as a way of establishing social order in the face of extreme violence.

5 The gift-seat passage has occasioned much comment, much of which is unsatisfactory, although the referents in the passage can be turned into conundrums, as Howell D. Chickering Jr, Beowulf. A Dual-Language Edition (New York, 1977), p. 287, nicely indicates. However, arguing in part on cultural grounds, Chickering takes the gift-seat as Hrothgar's and would have it and possibly treasure inside it protected by Hrothgar's divine mana if not by God Himself (p. 288). Margaret Pepperdene, 'Grendel's Geis,' Journal of the Royal Society of Antiquarians of Ireland 85 (1955), 188–92, is cited as thinking that the limit to Grendel's powers is a sign of hope, although not known as such to the Danes. Fred Robinson would have the lines say that Grendel was not compelled by God to show respect for the gift-seat, a reading possible but only outside of Beowulf for usages of 'gretan,' 'moste,' and 'for.' Moreover, the criminal and monstrous guest context is not that way well served. See 'Why Is Grendel's Not Greeting the Gifstol a Wræc Micel,' in Words, Texts and Manuscripts: Studies in Anglo-Saxon Culture Presented to Helmut Gneuss on the Occasion of His Sixty-Fifth Birthday, ed Michael Korhammer, pp. 257–62 (Cambridge, 1992).

6 See Alain Renoir, 'Point of View and Design for Terror in Beowulf,' in The Beowulf Poet, ed. Donald K. Fry, pp. 154–66. Renoir adds a sensitivity to cinematic effects and points of view to Arthur G. Brodeur's analysis of Grendel's approach — see The Art of Beowulf (Berkeley, 1960), p. 91. For irony of expectation at Grendel's expense, see Richard N. Ringler, 'Him seo wen geleah: The Design for Irony in Grendel's Last Visit to Heorot,' in Interpretations of Beowulf,' ed. R.D. Fulk, pp. 127–45. Also, for an exposition of Grendel as a nightmarish horror, we should note Michael Lapidge, 'Beowulf and the Psychology of Terror,' in Heroic Poetry in the Anglo-Saxon Period, eds. Helen Damico and John Leyerle, pp. 373–402 (Kalamazoo, 1993).

7 Kenneth R. Brooks, ed. Andreas and the Fates of the Apostles (Oxford, 1961), ll. 283b–284.

8 In an unpublished paper, 'The Translation of Conversation: Saintly and Heroic Modes of Speech in the Acta Andreae / Andreas,' Tom Shippey provides a kind of game-playing, favour seeking and giving version of these exchanges, where one can lose points but then regain social position as well: Andreas's lack of funds puts him at risk of losing social position; Christ could exploit that but does not. However, on the matter of no provisions, Christ is assertive, which provokes Andreas's sharp reply where

one maxim and further implication match another set. Christ's 'you're a fool' finds a match more strongly implied in Andreas's 'you're a boor.' Christ then has to apologize without 'going one down in his turn,' which he manages through a series of conditionals about who Andreas is and what he has been divinely commanded to do – on the terms of which he will take Andreas and his men aboard.

9   Theodore M. Andersson, 'Sources and Analogues,' in Bjork and Niles, eds., *A Beowulf Handbook*, pp. 125–48, at p. 139 (Lincoln, 1997). Nineteenth-century editors and translators such as John Kemble, Benjamin Thorpe, and John Earle are among early scholars who point to Telemachus's receptions when visiting Nestor or Menelaus and to Odysseus's arrival among the Phaeacians. H. Munroe Chadwick and W.P. Ker carry such observations toward and into the twentieth century. See Chadwick, *The Heroic Age* (Cambridge, 1912), p. 322; Ker, *Epic and Romance* (London, 1908), pp. 10–11. But one might add parallels from various places in both Homeric poems, such as the embassy to Achilles in Book IX of *The Iliad* where Achilles in order answers points set out in Odysseus's speech and where the idea that men distinguish themselves both by fighting well and speaking well appears in Phoenix's reply to Achilles. Then there is the ever present danger, despite divine preparations, that something Priam says will spur Achilles's anger, who even in defiance of Zeus might then kill his suppliant guest, Priam.

10   Carolyn Anderson, 'Gast, Gender and Kin in *Beowulf*,' *Heroic Age* 5 (Summer/Autumn 2001), electronic page six at http://www.mun.ca/mst/heroicage/issues/5/Anderson1.html. The quotations in Anderson's paragraph are from James Redfield, *Nature and Culture in the Iliad* (Chicago, 1975), p. 198, and Sheila Murnaghan, *Disguise and Recognition in the Odyssey* (Princeton, 1987), p. 76.

11   *Homer: The Odyssey*, trans. Robert Fagles (New York, 1996), Book 3, lines 80–3.

12   Ibid., Book 7, lines 274–6.

13   Ingeborg Schrobler notes some of these arrival similarities between *Beowulf* and *The Odyssey* in the course of gathering together many parallels of diction and phrasing for kings, warriors, sea-faring, ideas of divinity, and fate. Some of his parallels are indifferent ones, suggesting general similarities in the kinds of worlds and actions the poems dramatize. For the apparently notable number of parallels, Schrobler offers several possible explanations: the Anglo-Saxon poet knew Homer's poem; there is some intermediate source or sources between the two; Germanic heroic poetry has in general at some time been influenced by Homeric poetry;

or else the poems are totally independent, parallel developments. He seems to favour the last possibility – that is, parallel heroic ages – but is indecisive about that, perhaps because much of his research has been an investigation of the extent of Greek known in Anglo-Saxon contexts. See 'Beowulf und Homer,' *Beitrage zur Geschichte der deutschen Sprache und Literatur* 63 (1939), 305–46; especially 314–15 and 322.

14 *The Odyssey*, trans. Fagles, ll. 524 and following.

15 Ibid., ll 650–64.

16 See Thomas Shippey's excellent, detailed overview of these matters: 'Structure and Unity,' in Bjork and Niles, eds., *A Beowulf Handbook*, pp. 149–74 (Lincoln, 1997).

17 Andy Orchard, *A Critical Companion*, p. 103, n. 35, suggests that the expected *Beow* in line 53, which would fit metrically – according to Robert Fulk, 'An Eddic Analogue to the Scyld Scefing Story,' *Review of English Studies* 40 (1989), 313–22, at 314, n. 4 – is a scribal anticipation of the poem's hero, Beowulf.

2. Beowulf's Sudden Arrival and Danish Challenges: Nothing Said Is Merely a Formality

1 See Margaret W. Pepperdene, 'Beowulf and the Coast-guard,' *English Studies* 47 (1966), 409–19. For this and many other encounters, Martin Puhvel has speculated interestingly about the motivations of the characters involved, here thinking of the coastguard as showing heroic good manners in his 'starry-eyed' praise of Beowulf's appearance, which might temporize his earlier 'consternation' over the Geats' sudden landing. Moreover, there is simply good advice in his noting that should the Geats proceed inland without identifying themselves they would as a matter of course be considered legally as spies. Puhvel, *Cause and Effect in Beowulf* (Lanham, MD, 2005, p. 6, n. 2). There is, however, too much of modern, middle-class character motivation in Puhvel's speculations, and too little attention is given to an archaic world and its key terms and dangers.

2 T.A. Shippey, 'Principles of Conversation in Beowulfian Speech,' in John M. Sinclair, Michael Hoey, and Gwyneth Fox, eds., *Techniques of Description: Spoken and Written Discourse: A Festschrift for Malcolm Coulthard*, pp. 109–26 (London, 1993). That same intensity of thought will afflict Hygelac upon Beowulf's return to the Geats.

3 Shippey, 'Principles of Conversation,' pp. 120–1.

4 Robert Bjork ('Speech as Gift,' pp. 1009–11) masterfully describes the

rhetorical features of these two speeches – the coastguard's challenge and Beowulf's reply – noting that Beowulf's response 'generally conforms to the template his challenger has established.' Moreover, 'Beowulf's formal courtesy, his direct replies to direct questions about origins and intentions, and the resultant openness of the speech ... defuse the confrontation, which could have ended in mortal combat' (p. 1011). On the latter point I have to elaborate. Beowulf's eloquence, his use of alliterative enjambment and small-scale chiastic and framing patterns, no doubt helps him, but, crucially, his stress on his *ethical* posture toward Hrothgar is the key agent of defused tension here. His statement of intention has to find the right word – and he does in 'hold.' Edward B. Irving, Jr, *A Reading of* Beowulf (New Haven, 1968), pp. 52–5, expands on the idea of 'openness' as consummate tact, noting that Beowulf appeals to the coast watch for advice, admits that the rumours about Grendel might be wrong, and presents himself 'as a well-meaning adviser to Hrothgar' (p. 53). Moreover, 'Beowulf must not only disarm the Danes' hostility; he must gain acceptance from them, and gain it from *each individual* [emphasis mine] he encounters' (p. 53). That social necessity essentially sets up a pulse of arrivals, challenges, and responses, which in turn generates further social drama. See also Richard Barton Palmer, 'The Moral Portrait of the Hero,' Yale University dissertation, 1973, for a clause-based, studied account of Beowulf's exchanges with the coastguard, Wulfgar, Hrothgar and Unferth – mainly for points of similarity or contrast in characterizations of daring. Palmer thinks of the coast watch as astonished that Beowulf should come as he does rather than as worried, voicing then the possibility of aggressive response to possible threat (pp. 26–7, 89).

5 D.H. Green, *The Carolingian Lord: Semantic Studies on Four Old High German Words: Balder, Frô, Truhtin, Hêrro* (Cambridge, 1965), pp. 302–6.

6 George Clark, *Beowulf* (Boston, 1990), has economically shown some of the tensions and the respect involved in the coast watch's challenge; he shows no fear and his militarily prudent courtesies 'are those of an age of violence and nobility.' Moreover, he betrays no uneasiness about 'face' given Beowulf's arrival and stated intentions concerning Grendel (pp. 54–5). Wulfgar's reactions are, according to Clark, focused more on Beowulf's bravery; his anxieties, according to Clark, focus on the possibility that Hrothgar might not admit this warrior and his comrades (p. 55).

7 Andy Orchard, *A Critical Companion*, p. 211.

8 Ibid.: 'Apart from underlining Hrothgar's status ... Wulfgar's speech is intended to highlight Beowulf's own role: "since you are a petitioner" (*swa þu bena eart*, line 352b).' I would only add that Wulfgar does not make Beowulf's petitioner status his *only* role, as evident when he addresses Hrothgar, noting Beowulf's promising stature as a warrior and war-band leader.

9 Marshall Sahlins, *Islands of History* (Chicago, 1985).

10 Helen Damico, Beowulf's *Wealhtheow and Valkyrie Tradition* (Madison, 1984), p. 167.

11 Damico, Beowulf's *Wealhtheow*, p. 171; Francis P. Magoun, Jr, 'On the Old Germanic Altar- or Oath-Ring (*Stalla-hringr*),' *Acta Philologica Scandinavica* 20 (1949), 277–93.

12 Charlotte Behr, 'The Origins of Kingship in Medieval Kent,' *Early Medieval Europe* 9 (2002), 25–52.

13 Wealhtheow, having gone missing after sitting down, has been noticed by a few readers – beginning especially with Karl Müllenhoff, who uses it and other apparent lapses as part of his argument for an incompetent stitching of interpolations by a fifth author. See Tom Shippey's discussion, 'Structure and Unity,' p. 155. To have Wealhtheow exit regally would have distracted from the drama of the passing on of the hall, weakening its tight focus.

14 Much of the following discussion comes from my 'Translating Social Speech and Gesture in *Beowulf*,' in Beowulf *in Our Time: Teaching* Beowulf *in Translation*, ed. Mary K. Romsey, Old English Newsletter, Subsidia, vol. 31 (Kalamazoo, 2002), pp. 67–79, especially 70–2 and 77.

15 P.B. Taylor, 'Hrothgar and the Friends of Yng,' Hrothgar and Wealhtheow perform a 'ceremony of reinvestiture' in their 'extraordinary pageant' as they come into the hall (pp. 104–5), *Sharing Story* (Brooklyn, NY, 1998).

16 David Day, 'Jurisdiction and Justice in *Beowulf*,' University of Houston dissertation, 1992, pp. 93–4.

17 Ruth P.M. Lehman, *Beowulf: An Imitative Translation* (Austin, 1988).

18 John Josias Conybeare, *Illustrations of Anglo-Saxon Poetry*, Brooklyn, NY, 1964, p. 45.

19 One wonders in this connection whether Beowulf later comes upon Daeghrefn and his war band, disarms the champion, and then crushes him to death.

20 Francis B. Gummere, *The Oldest English Epic: Beowulf, Finnsburg, Waldere, Deor, Widsith, and German Hildebrand* (New York, 1909); R.K. Gordon, Beowulf in *Anglo-Saxon Poetry* (London, 1954).

21 Tolkien, 'On Translating Beowulf,' in *The Monsters & the Critics and Other Essays* (New York, 1997), p. 54.
22 Tolkien, 'Essays,' p. 55.

3. The Arrival of Joy after Grendel's Departure, and a Momentous Question: Succession or Not?

1 Hrothgar's thanking of God is a way of suggesting that this trophy is god-given, to him – not just a sight to behold.
2 The highly public nature of his giving enlarges its regality; the martial and dynastic character of his gifts makes their bestowal upon Beowulf a stunning, awesome act. No wonder the poet speaks in superlatives: never has he heard of a 'friendlier' giving, or a less shameful one (11. 1026–9).
3 Mary Dockray-Miller, 'Beowulf's Tears of Fatherhood,' *Exemplaria* 10.1 (1999), 1–28.
4 Scott DeGregorio, 'Theorizing Irony in *Beowulf*: The Case of Hrothgar,' *Exemplaria* 11.2 (1999), 309–43; especially 315–16, n. 26, and 333.
5 Sahlins, *Islands*, p. 90.
6 Sahlins, *Islands*, p. 90–1. I am especially indebted here to Sahlins for the notion that the martial son in some way softens the martial father.
7 Robert E. Kaske, '*Sapientia et Fortitudo* as the Controlling Theme of *Beowulf*,' *Studies in Philology* 55 (1958), 423–56.
8 John M. Hill, 'Beowulf and the Danish Succession: Gift-Giving as an Occasion for Complex Gesture,' *Medievalia et Humanistica*, n.s. 11 (1982), 177–97.
9 P.B. Taylor, 'Hrothgar,' [*Sharing Stories*,] 104–5.
10 Shippey, 'Principles of Conversation,' pp. 114–15.
11 Ibid., p. 120.
12 See Jane Chance, 'The Structural Unity in *Beowulf*: The Problem of Grendel's Mother,' in Helen Damico and Alexandra Hennessey Olsen, eds., *New Readings on Women in Old English Literature*, pp. 248–61 (Bloomingdale, 1990), on the possible parody of sexual relationships and of inverted hospitality(?) Homer has had Odysseus suffer the sexual attentions of goddess-hosts, who keep him against his inclinations (Circe especially comes to mind). See also Edward Irving, *Rereading Beowulf* (Philadelphia, 1989), p. 150, for comment on ironic hospitality here. Martin Puhvel (*Cause and Effect*) notes E.G. Stanley, 'Did Beowulf Commit *Feaxfeng* against Grendel's Mother?' *Notes & Queries* 221 (1976), 339–40. Hair-pulling, he adds, is a criminal offence in Æthelbert of Kent's legal code (it is a wergild offence having to do with bodily

injury). Moreover, Puhvel thinks that possibly the hair Beowulf pulls, if he pulls hair, is pubic (given differences in height or just crude scorning?). The manuscript clearly reads 'eaxle,' shoulder, but metrical arguments might weigh in for an emendation to 'feaxe,' a notion that A.J. Wyatt thinks, in a note on line 1537 and agreeing with William Morris, debases Beowulf's character, turning the match into a hag's brawl. See *Beowulf and the Finnsburg Fragment* (Cambridge, 1914). Although quite formidable, Grendel's mother is female and perhaps fighting a female is just less than manly, no matter how difficult or taxing the circumstances. After all, we have already been told that her battle terror is less than Grendel's even as a woman's is less than an armed man's. And Beowulf, having been hostily seized as an unwelcome guest, just might here deliberately insult his monstrous hostess, the short-term outcome of which is unfortunate for him as she somehow throws him and sits on him, intending his death.

13 For example, Irving, *A Reading of* Beowulf, p. 147.
14 'Tela,' well or properly, always occurs at the end of the b line and, except in 2663 (Wiglaf's urging on of Beowulf against the dragon), in a C verse; 'dugan' with the dative also occurs at the end of a b line.
15 Dockray-Miller, 'Tears,' p. 16; Shippey, 'Principles of Conversation.'
16 Shippey, 'Principles of Conversation,' p. 123.
17 See Susan Deskis, Beowulf *and the Medieval Proverb Tradition* (Tempe, 1996), pp. 126–7, on this important proverb. Similar sayings in Old Icelandic stories suggest that the strong and manly travel abroad whereas the timid stay home. Has Beowulf assessed a difference in character between the two princes?
18 Chickering, Beowulf: *A Dual-Language Edition* (New York, 1977); reprinted with Afterword (New York, 2006), p. 397.
19 Hrothgar's line is 'ge wið feond ge wið freond' (l. 1864a), a legalistic phrasing perhaps, as in VI Æthelstan, section 7: F.L. Attenborough edits the section, 'we wæron ealle swa on anum freondscype swa on anum feondscype, swa hwæðer hit þonne wære' ('we are all firm as one both in friendship and in enmity toward others, whichever it turns out to be'). (*The Laws of the Earliest English Kings* [Cambridge, 1922; reprinted in facsimile, Felinfach, 2000].)
20 Dockray-Miller, 'Tears,' p. 19.
21 John M. Hill, *The Anglo-Saxon Warrior Ethic: Reconstructing Lordship in Early English Literature* (Gainesville, 2000); see especially the introduction.
22 Dockray-Miller, 'Tears,' p. 19.
23 Ibid., pp. 23–4.

24 Thomas L. Wright, 'Hrothgar's Tears,' *Modern Philology* 65 (1967), 29–44, at 43.

25 Charles Plummer, *The Life and Times of Alfred the Great* (Oxford, 1902), p. 135.

26 Dockray-Miller, 'Tears,' p. 28.

27 Ibid., p. 28.

4. Beowulf's Homecoming with 'Celeritas' and Loyalty

1 See Seth Lerer, *Literacy and Power in Anglo-Saxon Literature* (Lincoln, 1991), pp. 187–91, especially where Beowulf as something of his own poet combines a 'historical account with entertaining story to tell us something of the function of literature in civilization' – which is 'the bringing together of an audience into a shared community and the demystification of the alien and supernatural.' Susan Marie Unter, 'Tales, Tellers and Audiences: Narrative Structure and Aesthetic Response in *Beowulf, Pearl, Cleanness, Patience,* and *Sir Gawain,*' University of California dissertation, 1984, suggests that the poet allows the hero 'to reflect the poet's narrative structure in his own mode of narration' (p. 51). An abstract analogy between word and referent and body and personal identity extends the language theme in Susan M. Kim's approach: Beowulf shows his language skill, but not to entertain; instead in the glove or pouch passage he 'represents ... his recognition and refusal of the consuming absence with which this language threatens him' – a difficult conception wherein Beowulf supposedly broods in a quasi-Augustinian way over sign and (necessarily absent or at least only conventionally attached) referent. See 'Boasting and Nostalgia in *Beowulf,*' *Modern Philology* 103 (2005): 4–27, at 16. Also Robin Waugh, 'Competitive Narrators in the Homecoming Scene of *Beowulf,*' *Journal of Narrative Technique* 25 (1995), 202–22, where Beowulf is seen to compete in the return home scene with the *Beowulf* poet's narration of events in and outside of Heorot. Recently Frederick M. Biggs, 'The Politics of Succession in *Beowulf* and Anglo-Saxon England,' *Speculum* 80 (2005), 709–41, departs from such readings to stress a political assertiveness on Beowulf's part, who pressures Hygelac in effect to reward Beowulf as handsomely as Beowulf has received or gotten rewards for himself from Hrothgar. We differ significantly in how we read Beowulf's gestures, his retainer diplomacy.

2 See Kenneth Sisam, *The Structure of* Beowulf (Oxford, 1965), p. 49; Klaeber, ed., *Beowulf,* p. 195; cvi; Gillian Overing, *Language, Sign and Gender* (Carbondale, 1990), p. 106; Marijane Osborn, '"The Wealth They

Left Us": Two Women Author Themselves Through Others' Lives in
Beowulf,' Philological Quarterly, 78 (1999), 49–76, is an exception as she
argues that Hygd appropriates this story for herself, weighing up its
meaning.

3 Seamus Heaney, *Beowulf: Bilingual Edition* (New York, 2000); Gummere,
The Oldest English Epic, 1909; G.N. Garmonsway and Jacqueline Simpson,
Beowulf and its Analogues (London, 1968). Martin Puhvel (*Cause and Effect*)
overlooks the intensity involved here as he thinks mainly of Hygelac's
'hearty' welcome, putting Hygelac's revelation of earlier concern about
his 'vassal's' voyage down to the likelihood of family solicitude, perhaps
fear of losing a valued retainer. Or he may not highly estimate Beowulf's
fighting skills (p. 70). Beowulf's 'deaf ear' to Hygelac's entreaty reflects
his *summum bonum*, pursuit of heroic glory. However, Beowulf is no
vassal, Hygelac is intensely curious, and while glory matters, the ethical
pull of Hrothgar's 'need' initially matters as much or more.

4 Frederick Biggs, 'Politics of Succession,' pp. 726–8, would read Beowulf's
phrase as a Norse-like self-judgment, which force the phrase certainly
has in an ironic context in *The Battle of Maldon*. But in *Beowulf* it has more
to do with a sense of free taking, which is Beowulf' s implication – no
obligations attached.

5 See my 'The Ethnopsychology of In-Law Feud and the Remaking of
Group Identity in *Beowulf*: The Cases of Hengest and Ingeld,' *Philological
Quarterly* 78 (1999), 97–124.

5. The Dragon's Arrival and Beowulf's Two Departures: Deep Luck Runs Out

1 Edward B. Irving, Jr, *Rereading* Beowulf, p. 107.

2 See Irving (ibid.) for a more poignant view: 'Though he walks toward the
dragon-barrow because he loves his people, he walks alone, to die alone,
to move temporarily outside the bounds of community toward a final
sacrificial solitude' (p. 110). Also, note Laurence N. De Looze, 'Frame
Narratives and Fictionalization: Beowulf as Narrator,' in *Interpretations of
Beowulf*, ed. Robert D. Fulk, pp. 242–50 (Bloomington, 1991). De Looze
thinks of Beowulf as trying to find first a historical and then a fictional
analogy (the case of the grieving father over his executed son) suitable
for his dilemma – that he must face the dragon but should he not, should
he be passive, who will? And should he die, what about his people and
their vulnerability to Swedes and Frisians? De Looze does not think of
Beowulf as in any special way addressing his retainers; indeed De Looze

thinks Beowulf may harbour some suspicion that they are cowards (p. 248, n. 9).

3 Bjork, 'Speech as Gift,' p. 1014.

4 To hear criticism in 'dollic,' as Andy Orchard and a few others do (see *A Critical Companion*, pp. 262–3) is sensible given the word's provenance in the poem (cf. 'dolgilp,' 'dolsceaða'). But the unusual sense of 'daring' that Klaeber offers has weight, given 'mærðo' in the preceding line. That word overwhelmingly denotes glorious, brave deeds in the poem, and both it and 'dollic' genitively modify deeds here.

5 See Richard Abels, '"Cowardice" and Duty in Anglo-Saxon England,' *Journal of Medieval Military History* 4 (2006). Apparently the Anglo-Saxons have no word for what we mean by 'cowardice,' that is, no concept much like ours.

6 By ending on what Swedes will do when they learn of Beowulf's death, the messenger, when then urging the Geats to hasten and see the doleful wonder of dead king and dragon, 'must be implying that they have to hurry; with the enemy at the gates there is little time [to organize themselves for] ... self-defense and the carrying out of the funeral rites' (*Rereading* Beowulf, p. 121).

7 Bjork, 'Speech as Gift,' pp. 1014–16.

8 See Rolf Bremmer, 'The Importance of Kinship: Uncle and Nephew in *Beowulf*,' *Amsterdamer Beitrage zur Alteren Germanistik* 15 (1980), 21–38, for a differing view, where Wiglaf is thought to be Beowulf's sister's son.

9 James W. Earl, *Thinking about* Beowulf (Stanford, 1994). Also Peter Richardson, 'Point of View and Identification in *Beowulf*,' *Neophilologus* 81 (1997), 289–98, for an overview of just how, from 'the moment Wiglaf is introduced, we literally see things his way, and he alone among the thanes retains the capacity to act ... [which is] perhaps the clearest indication of the poet's tendency to turn his audience into thanes and Beowulf's thanes into an audience,' p. 296). Additionally, Andy Orchard states: 'there must be an element of criticism here, where the many suffer because of one extraordinary man ... and where in a sense Wiglaf takes on the voice of the poet, marvelling at a heroism that he cannot quite condone' (*A Critical Companion*, p. 263). Orchard, however, does not think the poem quite condemns Beowulf (at least not in the way Heremod meets condemnation). Still, with Wiglaf I don't think Beowulf's heroism is in any way second guessed here. The impact of great loss partly floats his comment (even the messenger seems to have blamed Hæðcyn for presumption – 'onmedlan' – in taking on the Swedes); a need for solidarity with the remaining Geat nobility motivates the rest.

10 See Heaney, *Beowulf*.
11 See John M. Hill, *The Cultural World in* Beowulf (Toronto, 1995), p. 103.

Conclusion

1 Simon Keynes and Michael Lapidge, *Alfred the Great. Asser's* Life of King Alfred *and Other Contemporary Sources* (Harmondsworth, 1983).
2 See Meany, 'Scyld Scefing and the Dating of *Beowulf,' Bulletin of the John Rylands University Library of Manchester* 75 (1989): 7–40; and Keynes and Lapidge, *Alfred the Great*, p. 93. Also, Richard Abels, *Alfred the Great: War, Kingship and Culture in Anglo-Saxon England* (London, 1998).
3 Keynes and Lapidge, *Alfred the Great*, pp. 106–7.
4 All of the sections discussed here and below can be found in Attenborough, *The Laws of the Earliest English Kings*.

Works Cited

Abels, Richard. *Alfred the Great: War, Kingship and Culture in Anglo-Saxon England*. London, 1998.
– '"Cowardice" and Duty in Anglo Saxon England.' *Journal of Medieval Military History*, 4 (2006): 3–49.
Anderson, Carolyn. 'Gast, Gender and Kin in *Beowulf*.' *Heroic Age* 5 (Summer/Autumn, 2001): http://www.mun.ca/mst/heroicage/issues/5/Anderson1.html
Anderson, Earl R. 'Formulaic Typescene Survival: Finn, Ingeld, and the *Nibelungenlied*.' *English Studies* 61 (1980): 293–301.
Andersson, Theodore. *A Preface to the Nibelungenlied*. Stanford, 1987.
– 'Sources and Analogues.' In *A* Beowulf *Handbook*. Eds. Bjork and Niles, pp. 125–48. Lincoln, 1997.
– 'Tradition and Design in *Beowulf*.' In *Old English Literature in Context*. Ed. Niles, pp. 90–106 and 171–2. Cambridge, 1980. Reprinted in *Interpretations of* Beowulf: *A Critical Anthology*. Ed. F.D. Fulk, pp. 219–34. Bloomington, 1991.
Attenborough, F.L. *The Laws of the Earliest English Kings*. Cambridge, 1922. Reprinted in facsimile by Felinfach, 2000.
Behr, Charlotte. 'The Origins of Kingship in Medieval Kent.' *Early Medieval Europe* 9 (2000): 25–52.
Biggs, Frederick M. 'The Politics of Succession in *Beowulf* and Anglo-Saxon England.' *Speculum* 80 (2005): 709–41.
Bjork, Robert E., and John D. Niles, eds. *A* Beowulf *Handbook*. Lincoln, 1997.
– 'Speech as Gift in *Beowulf*.' *Speculum* 69 (1994): 993–1022.
Bremmer, Rolf H., Jr, 'The Importance of Kinship: Uncle and Nephew in *Beowulf*.' *Amsterdamer Beitrage zur Alteren Germanistik* 15 (1980): 21–38.
Brodeur, Arthur G. *The Art of Beowulf*. Berkeley, 1960.

Brooks, Kenneth R., ed. Andreas *and The Fates of the Apostles*. Oxford, 1961.

Calder, Daniel, ed. *Old English Poetry: Essays on Style*. Berkeley, 1979.

Chadwick, H. Monroe. *The Heroic Age*. Cambridge, 1912.

Chance, Jane. 'The Structural Unity in *Beowulf*: The Problem of Grendel's Mother.' In *New Readings on Women in Old English Literature*, ed. Damico and Olson, pp. 248–61, Bloomington, 1990.

Chickering, Howell D. Jr. Beowulf*: A Dual-Language Edition*. New York, 1977. Reprinted with Afterword. New York, 2006.

Clark, George. *Beowulf*. Boston, 1990.

Conybeare, John Josias. *Illustrations of Anglo-Saxon Poetry*. Brooklyn, NY, 1964.

Crowne, David K. 'The Hero on the Beach: An Example of Composition by Theme in Anglo-Saxon Poetry.' *Neuphilologische Mitteilungen* 61 (1960): 362–72.

Damico, Helen. Beowulf's *Wealhtheow and the Valkyrie Tradition*. Madison, 1984.

Damico, Helen, and Alexandra Hennessey Olson, eds. *New Readings on Women in Old English Literature*. Bloomington, 1990.

Day, David. 'Jurisdiction and Justice in Beowulf.' University of Houston dissertation, 1992.

DeGregorio, Scott. 'Theorizing Irony in *Beowulf*: The Case of Hrothgar.' *Exemplaria* 11.2 (1999): 309–43.

De Looze, Laurence N. 'Frame Narratives and Fictionalization: Beowulf as Narrator.' In *Interpretations of* Beowulf: *A Critical Anthology*. Ed. R.D. Fulk, 242–50. Bloomington, 1991. Reprinted from *Texas Studies in Language and Literature* 26 (1984): 145–56.

Deskis, Susan. Beowulf *and the Medieval Proverb Tradition*.Tempe, 1996.

Dockray-Miller, Mary. 'Beowulf's Tears of Fatherhood.' *Exemplaria* 10.1 (1999): 1–28.

Dumézil, Georges. *L'heritage Indo-Europeen a Rome*. 4th edition. Paris: Gallimard, 1949.

Earl, James W. *Thinking about Beowulf*. Stanford, 1994.

Earle, John. *The Deeds of Beowulf*. Oxford, 1892.

Fagles, Robert, trans. *Homer: The Odyssey*. New York, 1996.

– *The Iliad*. New York, 1990.

Fulk, Robert D. 'An Eddic Analogue to the Scyld Scefing Story.' *Review of English Studies* 40 (1989): 313–22.

Garmonsway, G.N., and Jacqueline Simpson, trans. *Beowulf and Its Analogues*. London, 1968.

Georgianna, Linda. 'King Hrethel's Sorrow and the Limits of Heroic Action in *Beowulf*.' *Speculum* 62 (1987): 829–50.

Gordon, Robert K. *Beowulf.* In his *Anglo-Saxon Poetry Selected and Translated,* revised edition. London, 1954.

Green, D.H. *The Carolingian Lord: Semantic Studies on Four Old High German Words: Balder, Fro, Truhtin, Herro.* Cambridge, 1965.

Grønbech, Vilhelm. *Vor Folkeaet I Oldtiden.* 4 Vols. Trans. William Worster as *Culture of the Teutons.* 3 Vols. Oxford, 1931.

Gummere, Francis B. *The Oldest English Epic: Beowulf, Finnsburg, Waldere, Deor, Widsith, and the German Hildebrand.* New York, 1909.

Heaney, Seamus. *Beowulf: A New Verse Translation, Bilingual Edition.* New York, 2000.

Hill, John M. *The Anglo-Saxon Warrior Ethic: Reconstructing Lordship in Early English Literature.* Gainesville, 2000.

– 'Beowulf and the Danish Succession: Gift-Giving as an Occasion for Complex Gesture.' *Medievalia et Humanistica,* n.s. 11(1982): 177–97.

– *The Cultural World in* Beowulf. Toronto, 1995.

– 'The Ethnopsychology of In-Law Feud and the Remaking of Group Identity in *Beowulf*: The Cases of Hengest and Ingeld,' *Philological Quarterly* 78 (1999), 97–124.

– 'Translating Social Speech and Gesture in *Beowulf*.' In Beowulf *in Our Time: Teaching Beowulf in Translation.* Ed. Mary K. Ramsey, pp. 67–79. *Old English Newsletter, subsidia,* vol. 31, Kalamazoo, 2002.

Hume, Kathryn. 'The Theme and Structure of *Beowulf*.' *Studies in Philology* 72 (1975): 1–27.

Hunter, Susan Marie. 'Tales, Tellers and Audiences: Narrative Structure and Aesthetic Response in *Beowulf*.' U of California, Riverside, Dissertation, 1984.

Irving, Edward B., Jr. *A Reading of* Beowulf. New Haven, 1968.

– *Rereading* Beowulf. Philadelphia, 1989.

Kaske, R.E. '*Sapientia et Fortitudo* as the Controlling Theme of *Beowulf*.' *Studies in Philology,* 55 (1958): 423–56.

Kemble, John M. *A Translation of the Anglo-Saxon Poem of 'Beowulf'.* London, 1835.

– *The Anglo-Saxon Poem of Beowulf. The travelers song and the battle of Finnerburh.* London, 1833.

Ker, W.P. *Epic and Romance: Essays on Medieval Literature.* Reprinted New York, 1957.

Keynes, Simon, and Michael Lapidge. *Alfred the Great*: Asser's *Life of King Alfred and Other Contemporary Sources.* Harmondsworth, 1983.

Kim, Susan M. 'Boasting and Nostalgia in *Beowulf*.' *Modern Philology* 103 (2005): 4–27.

Klaeber, Frederick. *Beowulf and the Fight at Finnsburg*. 3d edition with two Supplements. Boston, 1950.

Korhammer, Michael, ed. *Words, Texts and Manuscripts: Studies in Anglo-Saxon Culture Presented to Helmut Gneuss on the Occasion of His Sixty-Fifth Birthday*. Cambridge, 1992.

Lapidge, Michael. '*Beowulf* and the Psychology of Terror.' In *Heroic Poetry in the Anglo-Saxon Period: Studies in Honor of Jess B. Bessinger*. Eds. Helen Damico and John Leyerle, pp. 373–402. Kalamazoo, 1993.

Lerer, Seth. *Literacy and Power in Anglo-Saxon Literature*. Lincoln, 1991.

Lehmann, Ruth P.M. *Beowulf: An Imitative Translation*. Austin, 1988.

Lionarons, Joyce Tally. '*Beowulf*: Myth and Monsters.' *English Studies* 77 (1996): 1–14.

Magoun, Francis P., Jr. 'On the Old Germanic Altar- or Oath-Ring (*Stalla-hringr*).' *Acta Philologica Scandinavica* 20 (1949): 277–93.

Meany, Audrey L. 'Scyld Scefing and the Dating of *Beowulf* – Again.' *Bulletin of the John Rylands University Library of Manchester* 75 (1989): 7–40.

Müllenhoff, Karl. 'Die innere Geschichte des *Beowulfs*.' *Zeitschrift fur deutches Alterum und deutsche Literatur* 14 (1869): 194–244.

Murnahan, Sheila. *Disguise and Recognition in the Odyssey*. Princeton, 1987.

Niles, John D. *Beowulf: The Poem and Its Tradition*. Cambridge, MA, 1983.

Orchard, Andy. *A Critical Companion to* Beowulf. Cambridge, 2003.

Osborn, Marijane. '"The Wealth They Left Us": Two Women Author Themselves Through Others' Lives in *Beowulf*.' *Philological Quarterly* 78 (1999): 49–76. Reproduced in *Heroic Age* 5 (Summer, Autumn, 2000).

Owen-Crocker, Gale R. *The Four Funerals in* Beowulf. Manchester, 2000.

Overing, Gillian R. *Language, Sign and Gender in Beowulf*. Carbondale, 1990.

Palmer, Richard Barton. 'The Moral Portrait of the Hero: A Study of Three Ethical Questions in "Beowulf".' Yale University dissertation, 1973.

Pepperdene, Margaret W. 'Grendel's *Geis*.' *Journal of the Royal Society of Antiquarians of Ireland* 85 (1955): 188–92.

– 'Beowulf and the Coast-guard.' *English Studies* 47 (1966): 409–19.

Plummer, Charles. *The Life and Times of Alfred the Great*. Oxford, 1902.

Puhvel, Martin. *Cause and Effect in* Beowulf. Lanham, MD, 2005.

Redfield, James. *Nature and Culture in the* Iliad. Chicago, 1975.

Renoir, Alain. 'Point of View and Design for Terror in *Beowulf*.' In *The Beowulf Poet: A Collection of Critical Essays*. Ed. Donald K. Fry, pp. 154–66. Englewood Cliffs, 1968.

Richardson, Peter. 'Point of View and Identification in *Beowulf*.' *Neophilologus* 81 (1997): 289–98.

Ringler, Richard N. '*Him seo wen geleah*: The Design for Irony in Grendel's

Last Visit to Heorot.' In *Interpretations of* Beowulf: *A Critical Anthology*. Ed. R.D. Fulk, pp. 127–45. Bloomington, 1991.

Robinson, Fred. 'Why Is Grendel's Not Greeting the *Gifstol* a *Wræc Micel*,' in *Words, Texts and Manuscripts: Studies in Anglo-Saxon Culture Presented to Helmut Gneuss on the Occasion of His Sixty-Fifth Birthday*, ed Michael Korhammer, pp. 257–62. Cambridge, 1992.

Rogers, H.L. 'Beowulf's Three Great Fights.' *Review of English Studies* n.s. 6 (1955): 339–55.

Sahlins, Marshall. *Islands of History*. Chicago, 1985, 1987.

Schrobler, Ingeborg. 'Beowulf und Homer.' *Beitrage zur Geschichte der deutschen Sprache und Literatur* 63 (1939): 305–46.

Shippey, T.A. 'Principles of Conversation in Beowulfian Speech.' In *Techniques of Description: Spoken and Written Discourse*. Ed. John M. Sinclair, et al., pp. 109–26. London, 1993.

– 'Structure and Unity.' In *A* Beowulf *Handbook*. Eds. Bjork and Niles, 149–74, Lincoln, 1997.

– 'The Translation of Conversation: Saintly and Heroic Modes of Speech in the *Acta Andreae/Andreas*.' Unpublished conference paper, 1995: International Congress on Medieval Studies, Kalamazoo.

Sisam, Kenneth. *The Structure of* Beowulf. Oxford, 1965.

Taylor, P.B. 'Hrothgar and the Friends of Yng.' In *Sharing Story*, pp. 104–5. Brooklyn, NY, 1998.

Thorpe, Benjamin. *The Anglo-Saxon Poems of 'Beowulf,' The Scop or Gleeman's Tale and The Fight at Finnesburg*. London, 1855.

Tolkien, J.R.R. *'Beowulf*: The Monsters and the Critics.' *Publications of the British Academy* 22 (1936): 245–95. Reprinted. Donald K. Fry, ed. *The 'Beowulf'-Poet: A Collection of Critical Essays*, pp. 8–56. Englewood Cliffs, 1968.

– 'On Translating Beowulf.' In *The Monsters & the Critics and Other Essays*. New York, 1997.

Unter, Susan Marie. 'Tales, Tellers and Audiences: Narrative Structure and Aesthetic Response in *Beowulf, Pearl, Cleanness, Patience*, and *Sir Gawain*.' University of California dissertation, 1984.

Waugh, Robin. 'Competitive Narrators in the Homecoming Scene of *Beowulf*.' *Journal of Narrative Technique* 25 (1995): 202–22.

Work, James A. 'Odyssean Influence in the *Beowulf*.' *Philological Quarterly* 9 (1930): 399–402.

Wormald, Patrick. *The Making of English Law: King Alfred to the Twelfth Century, I: Legislation and Its Limits*. Oxford, 1999.

Wright, Thomas L. 'Hrothgar's Tears,' *Modern Philology* 65 (1967): 39–44.

Wyatt, A.J. *Beowulf and the Finnsburg Fragment*. Cambridge, 1914.

Index

Toronto Old English Series

May 1/08